THE GREAT
BRITISH
QUIZ BOOK

Table of Contents

Section 1: UK Geography *5*

Section 2: UK History *18*

Section 3: The Royal Family *36*

Section 4: British Food & Drink *46*

Section 5: British Sayings & Slang *56*

Section 6: British Sport *66*

Section 7: UK Flora & Fauna *76*

Section 8: British Art & Literature *86*

Section 9: British Landmarks & Monuments *97*

Section 10: Famous Brits *110*

Section 11: British TV & Film *121*

Section 12: British Music *132*

Section 13: British Holidays & Celebrations *143*

Section 14: British Inventions *150*

Section 15: British World Records *160*

Section 16: British Guess The Year *167*

Section 17: UK Myths & Folklore *173*

Section 18: British Nostalgia *179*

Answers *185*

Section 1: UK Geography

1. Which is the highest mountain in the UK?
A) Scafell Pike
B) Snowdon
C) Ben Nevis
D) Pen y Fan

2. Which river is the longest in the UK?
A) River Severn
B) River Thames
C) River Trent
D) River Mersey

3. What is the capital city of Scotland?
A) Glasgow
B) Aberdeen
C) Edinburgh
D) Dundee

4. Which of the following is NOT a British Overseas Territory?
A) Gibraltar
B) Falkland Islands
C) Bermuda
D) Isle of Man

5. Which lake is the largest by volume in the UK?
A) Loch Ness
B) Windermere
C) Loch Lomond
D) Lough Neagh

6. What is the UK's most easterly point?
A) John o' Groats
B) Lowestoft Ness
C) Land's End
D) The Lizard

7. Which city is known as the 'Oil Capital of Europe'?
A) Manchester
B) Liverpool
C) Aberdeen
D) Leeds

8. Which is the largest national park in the UK?
A) Lake District
B) Yorkshire Dales
C) Snowdonia
D) Cairngorms

9. Stonehenge is located in which English county?
A) Cornwall
B) Wiltshire
C) Somerset
D) Surrey

10. What is the capital of Wales?
A) Cardiff
B) Swansea
C) Newport
D) Bangor

11. The River Cam runs through which British city?
A) Oxford
B) Cambridge
C) Norwich
D) Bath

12. The Pennines mountain range is known as the 'backbone of England'. Which of these areas does it NOT run through?
A) Derbyshire
B) Yorkshire
C) Northumberland
D) Kent

13. Which British city was famously associated with the Titanic's construction?
A) Southampton
B) Liverpool
C) Belfast
D) Glasgow

14. Which of the following islands is NOT part of the Channel Islands?
A) Guernsey
B) Jersey
C) Isle of Wight
D) Sark

15. What is the smallest country in the United Kingdom?
A) England
B) Scotland
C) Wales
D) Northern Ireland

16. Hadrian's Wall was built to mark the northern limit of which ancient empire's territory in Britain?
A) The Roman Empire
B) The Macedonian Empire
C) The Persian Empire
D) The Viking Kingdoms

17. The Giant's Causeway is a natural wonder located in which part of the UK?
    A) Scotland
    B) Northern Ireland
    C) Wales
    D) England

18. What is the name of the river that flows through Liverpool?
    A) River Thames
    B) River Mersey
    C) River Severn
    D) River Tyne

19. The Cotswolds are a range of hills in which part of England?
    A) The Midlands
    B) The North
    C) The Southeast
    D) The Southwest

20. The historic city of Bath is famous for its Roman-built what?
    A) Temples
    B) Baths
    C) Villas
    D) Markets

21. Which of these is a river flowing through the Welsh capital, Cardiff?
    A) River Teifi
    B) River Taff
    C) River Usk
    D) River Wye

22. How many countries does the UK consist of?
A) Two
B) Three
C) Four
D) Five

23. Which sea lies to the east of the UK?
A) The Irish Sea
B) The North Sea
C) The Atlantic Ocean
D) The Baltic Sea

24. Where in the UK is Land's End located?
A) Cornwall
B) Devon
C) Dorset
D) Somerset

25. What is the largest island in Scotland?
A) Isle of Arran
B) Isle of Skye
C) Lewis and Harris
D) Mainland, Shetland

26. The Isle of Skye is part of which Scottish archipelago?
A) The Hebrides
B) The Shetland Islands
C) The Orkney Islands
D) The Inner Hebrides

27. In which UK city would you find the Royal Mile?
A) Edinburgh
B) Cardiff
C) London
D) Manchester

28. Which English county is known as the 'Garden of England'?
A) Surrey
B) Kent
C) Essex
D) Sussex

29. Which of these areas is famous for its slate quarries and mining heritage?
A) The Lake District
B) Cornwall
C) The Peak District
D) Snowdonia

30. The Cheddar Gorge, the largest gorge in the UK, is found in which county?
A) Derbyshire
B) Somerset
C) Gloucestershire
D) Wiltshire

31. Which city is famous for its historic docks, the Beatles, and was European Capital of Culture in 2008?
A) Birmingham
B) Liverpool
C) Bristol
D) Newcastle

32. Loch Ness is located in which Scottish region?
A) Highlands
B) Lowlands
C) Grampian
D) Tayside

33. Which of these UK cities is NOT a capital of one of the UK countries?
A) Belfast
B) Edinburgh
C) Liverpool
D) Cardiff

34. What is the name of the strait that separates the Isle of Wight from mainland England?
A) Menai Strait
B) Solent
C) Pembrokeshire Strait
D) The English Channel

35. The UK shares a land border with which country?
A) France
B) Ireland
C) Belgium
D) Netherlands

36. Which of these cities is known for its historic castle and is the largest city in Scotland?
A) Glasgow
B) Edinburgh
C) Aberdeen
D) Dundee

37. The Peak District is a national park located in which part of England?
A) The North East
B) The North West
C) The South East
D) The East Midlands

38. Which river runs through the city of Manchester?
A) River Irwell
B) River Mersey
C) River Tyne
D) River Severn

39. The Jurassic Coast is a World Heritage Site located in which two English counties?
A) Devon and Cornwall
B) Dorset and Devon
C) Sussex and Hampshire
D) Kent and Essex

40. Snowdon, the highest mountain in Wales, is located in which national park?
A) Pembrokeshire Coast
B) Brecon Beacons
C) Snowdonia
D) New Forest

41. Which city does the River Severn NOT flow through?
A) Shrewsbury
B) Bristol
C) Cardiff
D) Gloucester

42. Which UK country is known for having a dragon on its national flag?
A) Wales
B) Scotland
C) England
D) Northern Ireland

43. The Peak District National Park is located in which English region?
A) The South West
B) The North East
C) The East Midlands
D) The North West

44. Which of these UK cities is NOT a national capital?
A) Belfast
B) Cardiff
C) Edinburgh
D) Liverpool

45. What is the name of the large estuary that the River Thames flows into?
A) The Wash
B) The Solent
C) The Humber
D) The Thames Estuary

46. Which Scottish city is famed for its annual arts festival, the largest in the world?
A) Edinburgh
B) Stirling
C) Glasgow
D) Aberdeen

47. Snowdonia National Park is located in which part of the UK?
A) England
B) Scotland
C) Wales
D) Northern Ireland

48. The Isle of Man is located in which body of water?
A) North Sea
B) Irish Sea
C) English Channel
D) Atlantic Ocean

49. What is the largest lake by surface area in the UK?
A) Loch Lomond
B) Windermere
C) Loch Ness
D) Lough Neagh

50. In which English county would you find Plymouth?
A) Devon
B) Cornwall
C) Somerset
D) Dorset

51. Which of these rivers is found in Northern Ireland?
A) River Bann
B) River Severn
C) River Trent
D) River Tyne

52. The UK's only land border is with which country?
A) France
B) Ireland
C) Belgium
D) Spain

53. Ben Nevis is located near which Scottish town?
A) Fort William
B) Inverness
C) Oban
D) Stirling

54. Which British city is famous for its historical shipyard and the Titanic's departure?
A) Bristol
B) Liverpool
C) Belfast
D) Southampton

55. The Cotswolds are primarily located in which English county?
A) Gloucestershire
B) Oxfordshire
C) Wiltshire
D) Somerset

56. Which of these English cities is NOT located in the county of Yorkshire?
A) Leeds
B) Sheffield
C) Manchester
D) York

57. Dartmoor National Park is in which English county?
A) Devon
B) Cornwall
C) Hampshire
D) Surrey

58. The historical city of Bath is located along which river?
A) Avon
B) Severn
C) Thames
D) Mersey

59. The Hebrides are divided into the Inner and Outer groups and are part of which UK country?
A) England
B) Wales
C) Scotland
D) Northern Ireland

60. The Clifton Suspension Bridge spans which river in Bristol?
A) Avon
B) Severn
C) Mersey
D) Thames

61. Which of these is NOT one of the Channel Islands?
A) Jersey
B) Guernsey
C) Isle of Man
D) Sark

62. The city of Cambridge is most famous for its?
A) Port
B) Industry
C) Cathedral
D) University

63. Which English county is known for its Jurassic Coast, featuring landmarks like Durdle Door and Lulworth Cove?
A) Devon
B) Dorset
C) Somerset
D) Hampshire

64. Hadrian's Wall was built across what is now known as which English county?
A) Durham
B) Cumbria
C) Lancashire
D) Northumberland

65. What is the traditional county town of Lancashire?
A) Lancaster
B) Preston
C) Blackpool
D) Blackburn

Section 2: UK History

66. What was the principal cause of the Peasants' Revolt in 1381?
    A) The Black Death
    B) High taxes
    C) The Hundred Years' War
    D) Viking invasions

67. Who was the English monarch during the Spanish Armada?
    A) Queen Elizabeth I
    B) King James I
    C) Queen Mary I
    D) Queen Victoria

68. The Magna Carta was signed in what year?
    A) 1215
    B) 1066
    C) 1415
    D) 1603

69. What historical event is Guy Fawkes Night associated with?
    A) The English Civil War
    B) The Gunpowder Plot
    C) The Restoration
    D) The Glorious Revolution

70. Which queen was known as the 'Virgin Queen'?
    A) Mary I
    B) Anne
    C) Elizabeth I
    D) Victoria

71. Who was the first Tudor monarch?
A) Henry VII
B) Henry VIII
C) Edward VI
D) Elizabeth I

72. The Battle of Hastings in 1066 was fought between which two claimants to the English throne?
A) Henry II and Thomas Becket
B) Richard the Lionheart and Saladin
C) Edward the Confessor and Harold II
D) Harold II and William the Conqueror

73. The 'Domesday Book' commissioned by William the Conqueror was completed in what year?
A) 1086
B) 1066
C) 1100
D) 1215

74. Who was the British Prime Minister at the start of World War II?
A) Winston Churchill
B) Neville Chamberlain
C) Clement Attlee
D) Stanley Baldwin

75. What was the main reason for Henry VIII's break with the Catholic Church?
A) Doctrinal disagreements
B) Desire for a male heir
C) Personal religious conviction
D) Influence from Protestant ministers

76. Which English king was executed in 1649 after the Civil War?
    A) Charles I
    B) Charles II
    C) James I
    D) James II

77. Who was known as the 'Iron Lady'?
    A) Queen Elizabeth II
    B) Angela Merkel
    C) Indira Gandhi
    D) Margaret Thatcher

78. The Act of Union 1707 united the kingdoms of England and which other country?
    A) Wales
    B) Scotland
    C) Ireland
    D) France

79. Which event in 1666 devastated London?
    A) The Great Plague
    B) The Great Fire
    C) The Norman Conquest
    D) The Glorious Revolution

80. What was the main crop failure that caused the Irish Potato Famine?
    A) Corn
    B) Wheat
    C) Potato
    D) Rice

81. The English Reformation began under which monarch?
A) Henry VII
B) Mary I
C) Edward VI
D) Henry VIII

82. Which British explorer is credited with the first recorded European contact with the eastern coastline of Australia?
A) Sir Francis Drake
B) James Cook
C) Walter Raleigh
D) John Cabot

83. What was the primary industry of the Industrial Revolution in Britain?
A) Coal mining
B) Textiles
C) Steel production
D) Shipbuilding

84. Who was the last monarch of the House of Hanover?
A) George III
B) George IV
C) William IV
D) Queen Victoria

85. What British naval victory ended Napoleon's hopes of invading Britain?
A) The Battle of Trafalgar
B) The Battle of Waterloo
C) The Battle of the Nile
D) The Battle of Agincourt

86. What did the Chartists campaign for in the 19th century?
A) Abolition of slavery
B) Women's suffrage
C) Workers' rights
D) Electoral reforms

87. Who was the first female police officer in Britain with full powers of arrest?
A) Edith Smith
B) Florence Nightingale
C) Millicent Fawcett
D) Emmeline Pankhurst

88. The Boer Wars were fought by Britain in which territory?
A) India
B) South Africa
C) Australia
D) New Zealand

89. What year did women over the age of 30 gain the right to vote in Britain?
A) 1918
B) 1928
C) 1938
D) 1948

90. The Stone of Scone was historically used in the coronation of monarchs of which country?
A) England
B) Scotland
C) Wales
D) Ireland

91. What was the official religion of England after the Elizabethan Religious Settlement of 1559?
A) Catholicism
B) Lutheranism
C) Anglicanism
D) Calvinism

92. Which conflict was the result of the Glorious Revolution?
A) The English Civil War
B) The War of the Roses
C) The Jacobite Rebellions
D) The Seven Years' War

93. Who was the first Prime Minister of Great Britain?
A) William Pitt the Younger
B) Robert Walpole
C) Benjamin Disraeli
D) William Gladstone

94. The British East India Company established its first Indian factory in which city?
A) Bombay
B) Calcutta
C) Madras
D) Surat

95. What was the main reason for the passing of the Reform Act 1832?
A) To extend the franchise to the middle classes
B) To abolish the slave trade
C) To improve working conditions
D) To grant independence to American colonies

96. Which British monarch was on the throne at the time of the American Declaration of Independence?
A) George II
B) George III
C) George IV
D) William IV

97. What was the primary reason for the English colonization of Australia?
A) Trade with Asia
B) Establishing a penal colony
C) Searching for gold
D) Spreading Christianity

98. Who was the leader of the Suffragettes?
A) Florence Nightingale
B) Elizabeth Fry
C) Queen Victoria
D) Emmeline Pankhurst

99. What important medieval document is celebrated as a cornerstone of British liberty?
A) The Bill of Rights
B) The Charter of Liberties
C) The Magna Carta
D) The Act of Settlement

100. Who was the last Stuart monarch?
A) James II
B) Anne
C) Mary II
D) William III

101. The 'Battle of Britain' in 1940 was fought primarily in what domain?
A) Land
B) Sea
C) Air
D) Espionage

102. What was the name of the ship that brought the Pilgrims to America in 1620?
A) The Mayflower
B) The Victory
C) The Beagle
D) The Endeavour

103. The War of the Roses (1455-1485) was a conflict between which two houses?
A) Lancaster and York
B) Tudor and Stuart
C) Windsor and Hanover
D) Plantagenet and Norman

104. Which document, signed by King John in 1215, was important in limiting the powers of the king?
A) The Charter of the Forest
B) The Bill of Rights
C) The Magna Carta
D) The Act of Supremacy

105. The 'Glorious Revolution' of 1688 led to the overthrow of which king?
A) James I
B) James II
C) Charles I
D) Charles II

106. Who was the first monarch of the House of Windsor?
A) Edward VII
B) Victoria
C) Elizabeth II
D) George V

107. The Battle of Agincourt in 1415 was a major English victory in which conflict?
A) The War of the Roses
B) The Anglo-Spanish War
C) The Napoleonic Wars
D) The Hundred Years' War

108. What was the name of the period of Puritan-led government following the English Civil War?
A) The Restoration
B) The Commonwealth
C) The Protectorate
D) The Interregnum

109. Who was the British Prime Minister at the end of World War II?
A) Winston Churchill
B) Clement Attlee
C) Neville Chamberlain
D) Anthony Eden

110. What name is given to the mass emigration of English Puritans to the Americas in the 17th century?
A) The Great Migration
B) The Puritan Exodus
C) The Mayflower Departure
D) The Pilgrim Voyage

111. The 'Black Death' arrived in England in which century?
A) 12th
B) 13th
C) 14th
D) 15th

112. The 'Battle of Bosworth Field' in 1485 ended which king's reign?
A) Richard III
B) Henry VII
C) Edward IV
D) Henry VI

113. Who was the main opponent of Queen Elizabeth I during the Spanish Armada of 1588?
A) Louis XIV
B) Philip II of Spain
C) Henry IV of France
D) Pope Alexander VI

114. The 'Acts of Union 1800' united the Kingdom of Great Britain with which other kingdom?
A) Ireland
B) Scotland
C) Wales
D) France

115. What was the religious movement initiated by John Wesley in the 18th century?
A) Puritanism
B) Methodism
C) Quakerism
D) Anglicanism

116. Who led the Scottish forces at the Battle of Bannockburn in 1314?
A) William Wallace
B) Edward Bruce
C) James Douglas
D) Robert the Bruce

117. The 'Corn Laws', repealed in 1846, were tariffs on what?
A) Textile imports
B) Local breweries
C) Cornish metals
D) Imported grain

118. Who was the mother of Queen Elizabeth I?
A) Anne Boleyn
B) Catherine of Aragon
C) Jane Seymour
D) Anne of Cleves

119. The 'Charge of the Light Brigade' occurred during which conflict?
A) The Crimean War
B) The Boer War
C) World War I
D) The Napoleonic Wars

120. Which king was known as the "Merry Monarch"?
A) Charles I
B) Charles II
C) James I
D) James II

121. Who composed 'Rule, Britannia!'?
A) Thomas Arne
B) George Frideric Handel
C) Edward Elgar
D) William Byrd

122. The 'Peasants' Revolt' in 1381 was led by whom?
A) Wat Tyler
B) Jack Straw
C) John Ball
D) Richard II

123. Who was the last Governor of Hong Kong before its handover to China in 1997?
A) Margaret Thatcher
B) Chris Patten
C) David Wilson
D) Prince Charles

124. Which structure was built to house the Great Exhibition of 1851?
A) The Crystal Palace
B) The British Museum
C) The Tower of London
D) The Houses of Parliament

125. The 'Domesday Book' was compiled under which king?
A) Edward the Confessor
B) Harold II
C) William the Conqueror
D) Henry I

126. Who was the first woman to sit as a Member of Parliament in the UK?
A) Nancy Astor
B) Margaret Thatcher
C) Constance Markievicz
D) Barbara Castle

127. The 'Treaty of Union' that led to the creation of the United Kingdom was signed in which year?
A) 1603
B) 1707
C) 1801
D) 1922

128. The 'Gunpowder Plot' of 1605 aimed to assassinate which king?
A) James I
B) Charles I
C) Henry VIII
D) Edward VI

129. Which British queen was known as the 'Virgin Queen'?
A) Mary I
B) Elizabeth I
C) Anne
D) Victoria

130. The 'Battle of Hastings' in 1066 was fought between William the Conqueror and which English king?
A) Edward the Confessor
B) Aethelred the Unready
C) Edmund Ironside
D) Harold Godwinson

131. What was the primary industry in which the 'Industrial Revolution' in Britain started?
A) Automobile
B) Steel
C) Textile
D) Coal Mining

132. Which British explorer is credited with the first circumnavigation of the globe in 1577-1580?
A) Sir Walter Raleigh
B) Sir Francis Drake
C) James Cook
D) John Cabot

133. The 'Battle of Flodden' in 1513 was a conflict between England and which other country?
A) France
B) Scotland
C) Spain
D) Ireland

134. The 'Chartist Movement' in the 19th century was aimed primarily at which issue?
A) Trade union rights
B) Women's suffrage
C) Abolition of slavery
D) Electoral reform

135. Who was the legendary leader of the Knights of the Round Table?
A) King Arthur
B) King Alfred the Great
C) King Harold II
D) Richard the Lionheart

136. The 'Peterloo Massacre' of 1819 occurred in which city?
A) London
B) Manchester
C) Birmingham
D) Liverpool

137. Which treaty recognized the independence of the American colonies from Britain?
A) Treaty of Versailles
B) Treaty of Paris
C) Treaty of Utrecht
D) Treaty of Ghent

138. The 'Penny Black', introduced in 1840, was the world's first what?
A) Daily newspaper
B) Public railway
C) Postage stamp
D) Steel warship

139. Who was the legendary outlaw associated with Sherwood Forest and the reign of Richard the Lionheart?
A) Robin Hood
B) Dick Turpin
C) Blackbeard
D) Captain Kidd

140. The 'Great Fire of London' happened in which year?
A) 1666
B) 1605
C) 1558
D) 1620

141. The 'Balfour Declaration' of 1917 expressed British support for a national home for the Jewish people in where?
A) Uganda
B) Argentina
C) Palestine
D) Sinai Peninsula

142. The 'Amritsar Massacre', which took place in India under British rule, occurred in what year?
A) 1919
B) 1947
C) 1857
D) 1922

143. What was the main catalyst for the 'Swing Riots' in the 1830s?
A) Political reform
B) Agricultural technology
C) Industrial wages
D) Urban poverty

144. The 'Opium Wars' of the mid-19th century were between Britain and which country?
A) India
B) China
C) France
D) Russia

145. Which British monarch is associated with the saying "I may be the queen, but I'm also a grandmother"?
A) Queen Elizabeth I
B) Queen Victoria
C) Queen Mary
D) Queen Elizabeth II

146. The 'Battle of Trafalgar' in 1805 saw the defeat of the French fleet by which British admiral?
A) Admiral Nelson
B) Admiral Drake
C) Admiral Jellicoe
D) Admiral Beatty

147. Who was the British Prime Minister at the start of the First World War?
A) David Lloyd George
B) Herbert Henry Asquith
C) Winston Churchill
D) Stanley Baldwin

148. The 'Reform Act of 1832' addressed representation in which British institution?
A) The monarchy
B) The judiciary
C) The House of Lords
D) The House of Commons

149. Who was known as the 'Iron Duke' for his role in the Napoleonic Wars?
A) Duke of Wellington
B) Duke of Marlborough
C) Duke of York
D) Duke of Kent

150. The 'Cliveden Set' was a group of influential people who were accused of being sympathetic to which ideology in the 1930s?
A) Communism
B) Fascism
C) Anarchism
D) Socialism

151. The 'Bloody Code' in the 18th and early 19th century Britain refers to what?
A) The criminal laws imposing harsh sentences
B) The battle strategies in the Napoleonic Wars
C) The censorship laws for the press
D) The tax codes imposed by the Crown

152. The 'Suez Crisis' of 1956 involved the nationalization of the Suez Canal by which country?
A) Israel
B) Egypt
C) France
D) Britain

Section 3: The Royal Family

153. What is the name of the Queen's residence in London?
A) Buckingham Palace
B) Windsor Castle
C) Kensington Palace
D) Balmoral Castle

154. Who is second in line to the British throne as of 2023?
A) Prince George
B) Prince William
C) Prince Charles
D) Prince Harry

155. Which university did Prince William attend?
A) University of Oxford
B) University of Cambridge
C) University of St Andrews
D) Imperial College London

156. Who was the first wife of Prince Charles?
A) Camilla Parker Bowles
B) Diana Spencer
C) Sarah Ferguson
D) Anne, Princess Royal

157. What is the title given to the heir apparent of the British throne?
A) Duke of Edinburgh
B) Duke of Cambridge
C) Prince of Wales
D) Earl of Chester

158. What event is celebrated on the second Saturday in June in honor of the monarch?
A) The Coronation Festival
B) The Royal Ascot
C) The Queen's Official Birthday
D) Remembrance Sunday

159. Which royal is known for establishing the Invictus Games?
A) Prince Philip
B) Prince Harry
C) Prince Andrew
D) Prince Edward

160. Where was Queen Elizabeth II when she found out she was queen?
A) London, England
B) Nairobi, Kenya
C) Edinburgh, Scotland
D) Paris, France

161. What is the name of Prince William and Catherine's first child?
A) Prince George
B) Princess Charlotte
C) Prince Louis
D) Prince Archie

162. Which Royal Family member competed in the Olympics?
A) Prince Philip
B) Princess Anne
C) Zara Phillips
D) Both B and C

163. What is the title of the Queen's youngest son?
A) Duke of York
B) Duke of Sussex
C) Earl of Wessex
D) Duke of Kent

164. Which college did Prince Harry attend?
A) Eton College
B) Harrow School
C) Sandhurst Military Academy
D) Gordonstoun

165. Who is the Queen's only daughter?
A) Princess Beatrice
B) Princess Eugenie
C) Princess Anne
D) Princess Charlotte

166. Who is known as the Queen Mother?
A) Queen Mary
B) Queen Elizabeth II
C) Queen Elizabeth
D) Queen Victoria

167. Who is married to Sophie Rhys-Jones?
A) Prince Edward
B) Prince Charles
C) Prince Andrew
D) Prince William

168. What is Prince Philip's title?
A) Duke of Edinburgh
B) Duke of Windsor
C) Prince Consort
D) King Consort

169. What is the name of Prince Harry and Meghan Markle's first child?
A) Albert Frederick Arthur George
B) James Alexander Philip Theo
C) Edward Charles Louis
D) Archie Harrison Mountbatten-Windsor

170. Which royal got married at Westminster Abbey in April 2011?
A) Prince Charles
B) Prince Harry
C) Prince William
D) Princess Anne

171. In which year did Queen Elizabeth II celebrate her Diamond Jubilee?
A) 2013
B) 2012
C) 2015
D) 2010

172. What was the name of the Queen's father?
A) King Edward VIII
B) King Edward VII
C) King George V
D) King George VI

173. Which royal residence is located in Norfolk?
A) Sandringham House
B) Balmoral Castle
C) Holyrood Palace
D) Clarence House

174. What title was given to Kate Middleton upon her marriage to Prince William?
A) Duchess of Cambridge
B) Duchess of Sussex
C) Duchess of York
D) Countess of Wessex

175. What name is given to the Queen's official birthday parade?
A) The Queen's Procession
B) The Royal Salute
C) The Changing of the Guard
D) Trooping the Colour

176. Which royal has a passion for environmental causes and climate change?
A) Prince William
B) Prince Harry
C) Prince Charles
D) Princess Anne

177. What initiative did Prince William and Prince Harry launch together in 2009?
A) The Royal Foundation
B) Invictus Games
C) Sentebale
D) Heads Together

178. Who was the monarch before Queen Elizabeth II?
A) King George V
B) King George VI
C) King Edward VIII
D) King Edward VII

179. Which royal was once the governor of the Church of Scotland?
A) The Duke of Edinburgh
B) The Duke of York
C) The Earl of Wessex
D) The Duke of Rothesay

180. How many children do Queen Elizabeth II and Prince Philip have?
A) Two
B) Three
C) Four
D) Five

181. What is the name of Prince William's second child?
A) Prince George
B) Princess Charlotte
C) Prince Louis
D) Prince Harry

182. What is the traditional title for the wife of the Prince of Wales?
A) Duchess of Cornwall
B) Princess Consort
C) Countess of Chester
D) Duchess of Rothesay

183. Which royal married a commoner, Sarah Ferguson?
A) Prince Edward
B) Prince Andrew
C) Prince Charles
D) Prince Philip

184. Which castle is the Queen's preferred weekend home?
A) Windsor Castle
B) Buckingham Palace
C) Sandringham House
D) Kensington Palace

185. Who is the patron of over 600 charities, military associations, professional bodies, and public service organizations?
A) Prince Philip
B) Queen Elizabeth II
C) Prince Charles
D) Prince William

186. Which royal is known for her colorful hats?
A) Duchess of Cambridge
B) Duchess of Cornwall
C) Queen Elizabeth II
D) Princess Anne

187. Who was the last Emperor of India and the first Head of the Commonwealth?
A) King George V
B) King George VI
C) King Edward VIII
D) Queen Elizabeth II

188. What is the royal family's surname?
A) Windsor
B) Tudor
C) Mountbatten-Windsor
D) Hanover

189. Which royal has a degree in art history?
A) Princess Eugenie
B) Duchess of Cambridge
C) Prince Charles
D) Princess Beatrice

190. Which royal is a trained helicopter pilot?
A) Prince Harry
B) Prince William
C) Prince Charles
D) Prince Philip

191. What was the name of the Queen Mother's castle in Scotland?
A) Dunrobin Castle
B) Glamis Castle
C) Balmoral Castle
D) Stirling Castle

192. Who is the oldest grandchild of Queen Elizabeth II?
A) Peter Phillips
B) Prince William
C) Prince Harry
D) Zara Tindall

193. What is the ceremonial title held by the eldest son of the monarch in Scotland?
A) Duke of Cambridge
B) Earl of Inverness
C) Duke of Rothesay
D) Duke of Kent

194. Which royal was born on 21 June 1982?
A) Prince William
B) Prince Harry
C) Prince George
D) Princess Beatrice

195. What is the name of the Queen's only sister?
A) Princess Margaret
B) Princess Anne
C) Princess Charlotte
D) Princess Diana

196. Which royal is the Countess of Snowdon?
A) Lady Sarah Chatto
B) Lady Helen Taylor
C) Sophie, Countess of Wessex
D) Serena Armstrong-Jones

197. Who was known for the phrase 'Annus Horribilis' referring to 1992?
A) Prince Philip
B) Queen Elizabeth II
C) Prince Charles
D) Princess Anne

198. What charity did Princess Diana famously support by walking through a landmine field?
A) The Halo Trust
B) UNICEF
C) Red Cross
D) Save the Children

199. Which royal has a Master's degree in Equestrian Psychology?
A) Zara Tindall
B) Princess Anne
C) Prince Edward
D) Lady Louise Windsor

200. What is the name of the Queen's father's brother, who abdicated the throne?
A) King George VI
B) King Edward VII
C) King Edward VIII
D) King George V

201. Which royal is associated with the 'Duchy of Cornwall'?
A) Prince William
B) Prince Harry
C) Prince Charles
D) Prince Philip

202. What prestigious award scheme was founded by Prince Philip in 1956?
A) The Prince's Trust
B) The Duke of Edinburgh Award
C) The Royal Foundation
D) The Prince Philip Scholarship

Section 4: British Food & Drink

203. What is a traditional British pudding made from suet, flour, and dried fruit?
A) Apple crumble
B) Spotted Dick
C) Bread pudding
D) Trifle

204. What is the main ingredient in a traditional Scotch broth?
A) Beef
B) Barley
C) Chicken
D) Potatoes

205. Which of these cheeses is traditionally used for a Welsh Rarebit?
A) Cheddar
B) Stilton
C) Brie
D) Camembert

206. What is the key ingredient in a Lancashire hotpot?
A) Chicken
B) Pork
C) Lamb
D) Beef

207. What type of pastry is used to make a Cornish pasty?
A) Puff pastry
B) Choux pastry
C) Shortcrust pastry
D) Filo pastry

208. What is traditionally served with haggis?
A) Mash and peas
B) Neeps and tatties
C) Carrots and swede
D) Chips and gravy

209. Which of these is NOT a traditional British ale?
A) Bitter
B) Mild
C) Stout
D) Lager

210. A Bakewell tart is flavored with which fruit?
A) Apple
B) Cherry
C) Strawberry
D) Raspberry

211. Which of these ingredients would you NOT typically find in a full English breakfast?
A) Black pudding
B) Chorizo
C) Baked beans
D) Tomatoes

212. Bubble and squeak is made by frying together leftovers from which meal?
A) Breakfast
B) Roast dinner
C) Afternoon tea
D) Christmas dinner

213. Which fish is most commonly used in fish and chips?
A) Cod
B) Salmon
C) Tuna
D) Mackerel

214. What is the name of the Scottish soup made with smoked haddock, potatoes, and onions?
A) Borscht
B) Gazpacho
C) Cullen Skink
D) Minestrone

215. Which of these is a traditional British dessert?
A) Tiramisu
B) Pavlova
C) Eton Mess
D) Profiteroles

216. What is clotted cream typically served with?
A) Cheese and crackers
B) Fish and chips
C) Scones
D) Roast beef

217. Which of these drinks is considered the national beverage of England?
A) Coffee
B) Tea
C) Beer
D) Cider

218. What flavor is a traditional Victoria sponge cake?
A) Chocolate
B) Lemon
C) Vanilla
D) Almond

219. Which of these is NOT an ingredient in a traditional Toad in the Hole?
A) Sausages
B) Yorkshire pudding batter
C) Onions
D) Pasta

220. What is the name of a traditional British Christmas dessert?
A) Christmas cake
B) Cheesecake
C) Pecan pie
D) Chocolate mousse

221. Which of these is NOT a British beer brand?
A) Fuller's
B) Greene King
C) Bass
D) Heineken

222. What is the key ingredient in a traditional Stargazy pie?
A) Apples
B) Cherries
C) Peaches or apricots
D) Pilchards or sardines

223. What is the term for a traditional afternoon tea sandwich without crusts?
A) Club sandwich
B) Panini
C) Hoagie
D) Finger sandwich

224. Which of these desserts is made with a custard base topped with caramelized sugar?
A) Apple pie
B) Crème brûlée
C) Banoffee pie
D) Sticky toffee pudding

225. Which type of meat is traditionally used in a Shepherd's pie?
A) Beef
B) Pork
C) Lamb
D) Chicken

226. Which British dish is traditionally eaten on Bonfire Night?
A) Fish and chips
B) Parkin
C) Bangers and mash
D) Beef Wellington

227. Laverbread is made from what?
A) Seaweed
B) Wheat
C) Liver
D) Potatoes

228. Which region is famous for its Stilton cheese?
A) Cornwall
B) Cheshire
C) Somerset
D) Leicestershire

229. A '99' is a type of what?
A) Pie
B) Cake
C) Ice cream
D) Sandwich

230. In which part of the UK is the Arbroath Smokie traditionally produced?
A) Scotland
B) Wales
C) Northern Ireland
D) England

231. What is a "Butty" commonly referred to in British cuisine?
A) A dessert
B) A sandwich
C) A biscuit
D) A pie

232. What is the traditional topping for a Melton Mowbray pork pie?
A) Ketchup
B) Gravy
C) Aspic jelly
D) Mustard

233. Which British dish is made by boiling meat, fish, or vegetables in stock with dumplings?
A) Stew
B) Casserole
C) Cobbler
D) Roast

234. What is the main spirit in a Pimm's Cup?
A) Whiskey
B) Gin
C) Rum
D) Vodka

235. What is the name of the British dessert consisting of sponge cake and fruit covered with layers of custard, jelly, and cream?
A) Pavlova
B) Tiramisu
C) Trifle
D) Charlotte

236. Which of these ingredients is traditionally NOT in a Cornish pasty?
A) Potato
B) Swede
C) Beef
D) Chicken

237. What would you find inside a Battenberg cake?
A) Cream and strawberries
B) Marzipan
C) Custard
D) Chocolate ganache

238. What is another name for a bread roll in the East Midlands of England?
A) Bap
B) Bun
C) Cob
D) Loaf

239. Which of these is a popular savory spread made from yeast extract and used in British cuisine?
A) Branston Pickle
B) Marmite
C) Peanut butter
D) Piccalilli

240. How is a 'Black Velvet' drink made?
A) Red wine and cola
B) Stout and Champagne
C) Vodka and coffee
D) Whiskey and chocolate liqueur

241. What is the name of the British savory pie filled with minced meat and mashed potato on top?
A) Cottage pie
B) Pot pie
C) Quiche
D) Tart

242. What type of food is 'Pease pudding'?
A) A cake
B) A jam
C) A soup
D) A savory spread

243. What is the main flavor in Earl Grey tea?
A) Jasmine
B) Mint
C) Bergamot
D) Chamomile

244. Which of these is a traditional Sunday roast accompaniment?
A) Yorkshire pudding
B) Spotted Dick
C) Scotch egg
D) Pork pie

245. What kind of sauce is traditionally served with roast beef in England?
A) Apple sauce
B) Mint sauce
C) Horseradish sauce
D) Cranberry sauce

246. How do you traditionally eat a scone?
A) Topped with butter
B) Dipped in chocolate
C) With clotted cream and jam
D) Plain with no toppings

247. Which of these is NOT a British cocktail?
A) Bramble
B) Pimm's Cup
C) Bloody Mary
D) Margarita

248. What type of British pie has a filling of syrup, breadcrumbs, and lemon juice?
A) Apple pie
B) Lemon meringue pie
C) Treacle tart
D) Sticky Toffee Pudding

Section 5: British Sayings & Slang

249. What does it mean if someone is "gobsmacked"?
A) Angry
B) Confused
C) Amazed
D) Hungry

250. What does "the bee's knees" refer to?
A) It's old-fashioned
B) It's excellent
C) It's confusing
D) It's scary

251. If a Brit tells you to "keep your pecker up," what are they saying?
A) Stay cheerful
B) Stay angry
C) Stay quiet
D) Stay focused

252. What does "skint" mean?
A) Excited
B) Bored
C) Broke
D) Tired

253. What does "knackered" mean?
A) Angry
B) Confused
C) Tired
D) Excited

254. If someone is "chuffed to bits," how do they feel?
A) Very pleased
B) Annoyed
C) Hopeful
D) Indifferent

255. What does "taking the mickey" mean?
A) Taking a break
B) Teasing or mocking someone
C) Taking a photograph
D) Taking responsibility

256. If something is described as "dodgy," what is it?
A) Suspicious or poor quality
B) Fast
C) Expensive
D) Delicious

257. What does the term "gutted" mean?
A) Excited
B) Devastated or very disappointed
C) Hungry
D) Confident

258. What does it mean to "have a gander"?
A) To have a dance
B) To have a fight
C) To take a quick look
D) To have a rest

259. If someone is "full of beans," what are they?
A) Angry
B) Drunk
C) Farting alot
D) Energetic

260. What does it mean if something "costs an arm and a leg"?
A) It's very cheap
B) It's affordable
C) It's preposterously priced relative to other similar items
D) It's very expensive

261. If someone is described as "a few sandwiches short of a picnic," what does it mean?
A) They are hungry
B) They are unprepared
C) They are not very intelligent or are behaving oddly
D) They are sad

262. What does "blimey" express?
A) Surprise
B) Curiosity
C) Anger
D) Disappointment

263. What does "bog-standard" mean?
A) High-quality
B) Ordinary, with no frills
C) Complicated
D) Dirty

264. What does "cheesed off" mean?
A) Happy
B) Annoyed
C) Confused
D) Excited

265. If a person is "brassed off," what are they?
A) Fed up
B) Proud
C) Cold
D) Impressed

266. If you're "on the pull," what are you doing?
A) Trying to find a romantic partner
B) Exercising
C) Financially struggling
D) In trouble for something

267. What does "pear-shaped" refer to?
A) Something going well
B) A type of dessert
C) Being overweight
D) Something going wrong

268. What is a "quid"?
A) A game
B) A quiet person
C) A type of British squid
D) British pound sterling

269. If something is "tickety-boo," how is it?
A) Confusing
B) In good order, going well
C) Beyond repair
D) Loud

270. What does it mean to "bunk off"?
A) To jump very high
B) To sleep
C) To skip an obligation, especially school
D) To dance

271. If someone tells you to "throw a spanner in the works," what do they mean?
A) Work harder
B) Cause a disturbance
C) Fix something
D) Start a new project

272. If someone is described as "the full monty," what does it mean?
A) They are fully dressed
B) They are very skilled
C) The whole thing, or everything that is possible
D) They are very serious

273. What does it mean if you are "cream crackered"?
A) You are very wealthy
B) You are very tired
C) You are excited
D) You are well-dressed

274. What does the phrase "Bob's your uncle" mean?
A) It's a way of saying you're related
B) It's a statement of job security
C) It's said when something is finished or completed easily
D) It's a warning about a person named Bob

275. If someone is "mad as a hatter," how are they behaving?
A) Calm and rational
B) Eccentric or crazy
C) Angry and violent
D) Sad and depressed

276. What does the expression "over the moon" mean?
A) Very happy
B) Very tired
C) Very confused
D) Very dreamy

277. What does "to nick" something mean?
A) To clean it
B) To steal it
C) To break it
D) To buy it

278. If you are "gutted," how are you feeling?
A) Ecstatic
B) Thirsty
C) Extremely disappointed
D) Ill

279. What does "to leg it" mean?
A) To dance
B) To exercise
C) To run away quickly
D) To tiptoe quietly

280. What does "chinwag" mean?
A) A type of dance
B) A nice beard
C) A serious debate
D) A casual conversation

281. What does "naff" mean?
A) Tasteless
B) In fashion
C) Stolen
D) New and exciting

282. If you're "feeling peckish," what are you feeling?
A) In an irritating mood
B) Starving
C) Cold
D) A little hungry

283. If you've made a "dog's dinner" of something, what have you done?
A) Made a mess of something
B) Eaten very quickly
C) Cooked a meal for a dog
D) Prepared a very fancy meal

284. If someone is described as being "on the fiddle," what are they doing?
A) Being dishonest or fraudulent
B) Working hard or being determined
C) Playing a musical instrument
D) Dancing

285. If you're told to "put a sock in it," what should you do?
A) Go to sleep
B) Stop talking or be quiet
C) Put your clothes away
D) Change your attitude

286. What does "waffle" mean in British slang?
A) A type of breakfast food
B) To speak or write lengthily and without making much point
C) To complain
D) To walk with a swaying motion

287. If someone has "lost the plot," what has happened?
A) They have forgotten what they were saying
B) They have stopped following a story or conversation
C) They have become irrational or are not thinking sensibly
D) They have misplaced a book

288. What does "sod's law" refer to?
A) Any cracks in the legal system
B) If one person does it, others are bound to follow
C) The idea that if something can go wrong, it will
D) A rule about property

289. If you've had "a bit too much to drink," you might be described as what?
A) Sloshed
B) Gabbered
C) Knackered
D) Wimpery

290. When a Brit says "I'm feeling ropey," what do they mean?
A) They are feeling very strong
B) They are feeling unwell or not quite right
C) They are feeling excited
D) They are feeling tied down

291. What does "the Old Bill" refer to?
A) Old currency
B) A former politician
C) The police
D) An old friend

292. If someone is "on their tod," what does that mean?
A) They are performing well
B) They are in trouble
C) They are alone
D) They are dressed formally

293. What does "gormless" mean?
A) Lacking intelligence
B) Clumsy
C) Fearless
D) Full of life

294. If a person "can't be arsed," what do they mean?
A) They can't sit down
B) They lack the will or desire to do something
C) They can't understand something
D) They are feeling constipated

295. What does it mean if you are "quids in"?
A) You owe money
B) You are very quiet
C) You have made a profit or are in a favorable position
D) You are feeling ill

296. When someone is "taking the biscuit," what are they doing?
A) Baking
B) Winning
C) Taking a risk
D) Pushing the limits of what is acceptable

297. What does "codswallop" mean?

A) An eating method for fish and chips

B) Nonsense

C) A compliment

D) A beer drank in one go

Section 6: British Sport

298. Who won Wimbledon Men's Singles title in 2013?
A) Roger Federer
B) Novak Djokovic
C) Andy Murray
D) Rafael Nadal

299. Which British city hosted the Commonwealth Games in 2002?
A) Glasgow
B) London
C) Manchester
D) Birmingham

300. Which team won the English Premier League in the 2019-2020 season?
A) Manchester City
B) Chelsea
C) Liverpool
D) Manchester United

301. Who is known as "The Flying Scotsman" in the world of cycling?
A) Chris Froome
B) Mark Cavendish
C) Sir Chris Hoy
D) Graeme Obree

302. In which year did London last host the Summer Olympics before 2012?
A) 1908
B) 1948
C) 1956
D) 1960

303. Who is England's all-time top goalscorer in football?
A) Bobby Charlton
B) Gary Lineker
C) Harry Kane
D) Wayne Rooney

304. Which British athlete won gold in the decathlon at the 1980 Moscow Olympics?
A) Daley Thompson
B) Mo Farah
C) Steve Ovett
D) Sebastian Coe

305. Where is the British Grand Prix Formula 1 race traditionally held?
A) Brands Hatch
B) Silverstone
C) Donington Park
D) Aintree

306. Who won the BBC Sports Personality of the Year Award in 2005?
A) Andrew Flintoff
B) David Beckham
C) Kelly Holmes
D) Joe Calzaghe

307. Which horse race is known as "The Grand National"?
A) Epsom Derby
B) Cheltenham Gold Cup
C) Aintree Grand National
D) Royal Ascot

308. What is the nickname of the English national rugby union team?
A) The Lions
B) The Red Roses
C) The Bulldogs
D) The Saxons

309. Who was the first British driver to win the Formula One World Championship?
A) Jackie Stewart
B) James Hunt
C) Lewis Hamilton
D) Mike Hawthorn

310. Which English football club is nicknamed "The Toffees"?
A) Everton
B) Chelsea
C) Tottenham Hotspur
D) Manchester City

311. How many times has the British and Irish Lions rugby union team won a series against New Zealand?
A) 0
B) 1
C) 2
D) 3

312. Who is the most successful British swimmer in Olympic history?
A) Rebecca Adlington
B) Adam Peaty
C) Duncan Goodhew
D) Anita Lonsbrough

313. Which venue in London is synonymous with tennis?
A) The O2 Arena
B) Queen's Club
C) Wimbledon
D) Lords

314. In cricket, who is England's highest Test run-scorer?
A) Joe Root
B) Alastair Cook
C) Kevin Pietersen
D) Ian Bell

315. Where are the Henley Royal Regatta rowing races held?
A) On the Thames in London
B) On the Thames in Henley-on-Thames
C) On the Severn in Shrewsbury
D) On the Mersey in Liverpool

316. Who won the Rugby Union World Cup with England in 2003?
A) Jonny Wilkinson
B) Martin Johnson
C) Lawrence Dallaglio
D) Jason Robinson

317. Which British golfer won The Open Championship in 1999?
A) Nick Faldo
B) Rory McIlroy
C) Paul Lawrie
D) Justin Rose

318. Who is the only British driver to win the Indy 500 more than once?
A) Dario Franchitti
B) Jim Clark
C) Graham Hill
D) Nigel Mansell

319. Which British boxer is known as the "Gypsy King"?
A) Anthony Joshua
B) Tyson Fury
C) Lennox Lewis
D) Joe Calzaghe

320. How many home nations are represented in the British and Irish Lions rugby union team?
A) 2
B) 3
C) 4
D) 5

321. What is the maximum break in snooker?
A) 147
B) 155
C) 150
D) 160

322. In what year did England's football team win the FIFA World Cup?
A) 1966
B) 1970
C) 1982
D) 1990

323. Who is the only English footballer to have won league titles in four countries?
A) David Beckham
B) Steven Gerrard
C) Frank Lampard
D) Wayne Rooney

324. Which British female athlete won two gold medals at the 2004 Athens Olympics?
A) Denise Lewis
B) Jessica Ennis-Hill
C) Kelly Holmes
D) Christine Ohuruogu

325. Which venue hosts the British Masters golf tournament?
A) St. Andrews
B) Wentworth Club
C) Walton Heath
D) The Belfry

326. Who is the most successful British Olympian in terms of gold medals won?
A) Sir Chris Hoy
B) Sir Steve Redgrave
C) Sir Mo Farah
D) Sir Bradley Wiggins

327. Which of these British athletes has never won an Olympic gold medal?
A) Greg Rutherford
B) Tom Daley
C) Dame Jessica Ennis-Hill
D) Sir Chris Hoy

328. Who captained the English rugby team to victory in the 2003 Rugby World Cup?
A) Jonny Wilkinson
B) Martin Johnson
C) Will Carling
D) Lawrence Dallaglio

329. Who is the most successful English club in Champions League history?
A) Manchester United
B) Liverpool
C) Chelsea
D) Nottingham Forest

330. Which British athlete is famous for their long-distance running achievements?
A) Paula Radcliffe
B) Steve Ovett
C) Sebastian Coe
D) Sir Mo Farah

331. At which racecourse is the St Leger Stakes run?
A) Ascot
B) Aintree
C) Doncaster
D) Newmarket

332. Who was the first English footballer to become a knight?
A) Bobby Moore
B) Sir Bobby Charlton
C) Sir Geoff Hurst
D) Sir Stanley Matthews

333. In what year did the London Marathon first take place?
A) 1970
B) 1981
C) 1990
D) 2000

334. What color jersey is worn by the leader of the Tour of Britain cycling race?
A) Yellow
B) Green
C) Polka dot
D) Blue

335. Which English footballer has the most international caps?
A) David Beckham
B) Peter Shilton
C) Wayne Rooney
D) Bobby Moore

336. Which of these venues has not hosted the Summer Olympic Games?
A) London
B) Manchester
C) Glasgow
D) All have hosted

337. In darts, what is the highest possible score with three darts?
A) 180
B) 190
C) 170
D) 150

338. Who was the first British woman to win an Olympic boxing gold medal?
A) Savannah Marshall
B) Katie Taylor
C) Nicola Adams
D) Natasha Jonas

339. In which year did England host the Rugby World Cup?
A) 1991
B) 1999
C) 2003
D) 2015

340. What is the name of the trophy awarded to the winners of the Ashes cricket series?
A) The Ashes Urn
B) The Imperial Cup
C) The Cricket Crown
D) The Test Trophy

341. Who was the youngest British Formula One driver to win a race?
A) Lewis Hamilton
B) Jenson Button
C) George Russell
D) Lando Norris

342. Which English football club is known as "The Blades"?
A) Sheffield United
B) Sheffield Wednesday
C) Bradford City
D) Birmingham City

343. Who has won more tennis Grand Slam titles, Andy
Murray or Fred Perry?
A) Andy Murray
B) Fred Perry
C) They have won the same number
D) Neither have won any

344. The Oxford and Cambridge Boat Race traditionally
takes place on which river?
A) River Thames
B) River Cam
C) River Isis
D) River Severn

345. Who was England's rugby head coach during the 2003
Rugby World Cup victory?
A) Clive Woodward
B) Eddie Jones
C) Martin Johnson
D) Geoff Cooke

346. What is the traditional name given to the Test cricket
series played between England and Australia?
A) The Great Cricket Battle
B) The Cricket Super Series
C) The Ashes
D) The Trans-Tasman Trophy

347. Which British athlete set a world record in the
marathon in 2003?
A) Paula Radcliffe
B) Mo Farah
C) Steve Cram
D) Jonathan Edwards

Section 7: UK Flora & Fauna

348. Which of the following trees is native to the UK?
A) Neem
B) Olive
C) Oak
D) Baobab

349. What is the largest land mammal native to the UK?
A) Grey Squirrel
B) Red Deer
C) European Badger
D) Hedgehog

350. Which British bird is known for its bright blue plumage and orange breast and cheeks?
A) Kingfisher
B) Goldfinch
C) Blue Tit
D) Robin

351. The Scottish Wildcat, native to Scotland, is closely related to which domestic animal?
A) Dog
B) Cat
C) Rabbit
D) Ferret

352. Which of the following plants is considered an invasive species in the UK?
A) Snowdrop
B) Bluebell
C) Japanese Knotweed
D) Foxglove

353. The Cuckoo Flower is also commonly known by what other name?
A) Lady's Smock
B) King's Crown
C) Duke's Mantle
D) Queen's Lace

354. Which of these is a butterfly native to the UK?
A) Monarch
B) Painted Lady
C) Swallowtail
D) Both B and C

355. What is the most common species of oak found in the UK?
A) Red Oak
B) White Oak
C) English Oak
D) Black Oak

356. The Common Frog is a usual sight in British gardens. What is its scientific name?
A) Rana temporaria
B) Bufo bufo
C) Hyla arborea
D) Anura gardenii

357. The Red Squirrel is native to the UK. What has caused their population to decline?
A) Habitat loss
B) Disease from Grey Squirrels
C) Predation by birds of prey
D) All of the above

358. Which of these birds is known for mimicking the calls of other birds?
A) Starling
B) Blackbird
C) Sparrowhawk
D) Nightingale

359. What kind of habitat is the Scottish crossbill specially adapted to?
A) Wetlands
B) Coniferous forests
C) Meadows
D) Heathlands

360. The Chalkhill Blue is a species of what?
A) Moth
B) Butterfly
C) Beetle
D) Dragonfly

361. Which of these mammals is a protected species in the UK?
A) Brown Rat
B) Fallow Deer
C) Water Vole
D) Red Fox

362. The Basking Shark is a seasonal visitor to British waters. What does it primarily feed on?
A) Fish
B) Plankton
C) Seals
D) Squid

363. Which of these is NOT a native UK species of woodpecker?
A) Great Spotted Woodpecker
B) Lesser Spotted Woodpecker
C) Green Woodpecker
D) Red-bellied Woodpecker

364. The Pasqueflower is a rare wildflower in the UK and is associated with what type of habitat?
A) Coastal cliffs
B) Chalk grasslands
C) Peat bogs
D) Woodland edges

365. Which species of bat is the most common in the UK?
A) Brown Long-eared Bat
B) Greater Horseshoe Bat
C) Common Pipistrelle
D) Grey Long-eared Bat

366. What is the primary diet of the European Hedgehog found in the UK?
A) Leaves and berries
B) Insects and worms
C) Small mammals
D) Fruits

367. What is the name of the only venomous snake native to the UK?
A) Corn Snake
B) Adder
C) Grass Snake
D) Smooth Snake

368. Which bird is known for its distinctive 'drumming' display during the breeding season?
A) Woodcock
B) Snipe
C) Grouse
D) Wood Pigeon

369. What distinctive feature does the male Capercaillie have during the breeding season?
A) Bright blue chest
B) Large antlers
C) Inflatable red throat pouch
D) Long tail feathers

370. The UK's native Bluebell is under threat from hybridization with which species?
A) Spanish Bluebell
B) American Bluebell
C) French Bluebell
D) Dutch Bluebell

371. The Mountain Hare changes color seasonally. What color is its coat in winter?
A) Brown
B) Grey
C) White
D) Black

372. What is the function of the large ears of the Brown Hare?
A) To detect predators
B) To regulate body temperature
C) For mating displays
D) Both A and B

373. Which of these plant species is known to be carnivorous?
A) Sundew
B) Bluebell
C) Cowslip
D) Snowdrop

374. The Hazel Dormouse is notable for what behavior in colder months?
A) Hibernation
B) Migration
C) Storing food
D) Burrowing underground

375. What is the primary diet of the Red Fox?
A) Plants and berries
B) Insects
C) Small mammals and birds
D) Fish

376. Which UK bird is famous for its elaborate courtship dance?
A) Black Grouse
B) Peacock
C) Mute Swan
D) Puffin

377. The Slow Worm found in the UK is actually what type of creature?
A) Worm
B) Snake
C) Lizard
D) Snail

378. What type of area would you most likely find a Dartford Warbler?
A) Wetlands
B) Heathland
C) Deciduous forest
D) Urban areas

379. The common toad is also known by what other name in the UK?
A) Water toad
B) Bufo toad
C) European toad
D) Garden toad

380. Which UK mammal has a diet that consists almost entirely of eels and fish?
A) Otter
B) Weasel
C) Stoat
D) Badger

381. The Silver-washed Fritillary is a type of what?
A) Bird
B) Butterfly
C) Fish
D) Moth

382. Which tree is known for its helicopter-like seed pods?
A) Ash
B) Sycamore
C) Beech
D) Oak

383. The Marsh Fritillary butterfly is dependent on what plant to survive?
A) Thistles
B) Nettles
C) Devil's-bit Scabious
D) Buttercups

384. What is a 'lek' in relation to British wildlife?
A) A small stream
B) A breeding display area for birds
C) A type of shelter built by otters
D) A deer's territory

385. Which animal introduced to the UK has a significant impact on the Red Squirrel population?
A) Grey Squirrel
B) American Mink
C) Canadian Beaver
D) Feral Goat

386. The UK's Large Blue butterfly has a unique relationship with what other species during its larval stage?
A) Ants
B) Bees
C) Wasps
D) Beetles

387. What characteristic feature distinguishes the male Common Pheasant from the female?
A) Size
B) Tail length
C) Color
D) All of the above

388. The UK's Nightjar is most notable for what behavior?
A) Migrating during the day
B) Singing at night
C) Eating while flying
D) Glowing in the dark

389. What is the primary food source for the Pine Marten?
A) Small rodents
B) Berries and fruits
C) Birds' eggs
D) All of the above

390. The European Badger is a member of which animal family?
A) Canidae (Dog family)
B) Ursidae (Bear family)
C) Mustelidae (Weasel family)
D) Felidae (Cat family)

391. What distinguishing feature does the Skylark have when in flight?
A) It hovers in place.
B) It has a distinctive song.
C) It flies in a figure-eight pattern.
D) It makes a loud clapping sound.

392. Which marine creature is known for its five-fold symmetry and can be found around the UK's coastlines?
A) Sea urchin
B) Starfish
C) Cuttlefish
D) Jellyfish

393. The UK's Bechstein's bat is primarily found in what type of habitat?
A) Urban areas
B) Broadleaved woodland
C) Moorland
D) Coastal areas

394. What is the main diet of the Stoat, a common UK carnivore?
A) Fish
B) Insects
C) Small mammals and birds
D) Fruits

395. The flower known as Ragged Robin is often found in which type of habitat?
A) Woodlands
B) Wet meadows
C) Heathlands
D) Coastal cliffs

396. The Sea Holly is a plant that thrives in what coastal feature?
A) Dunes
B) Rock pools
C) Cliffs
D) Salt marshes

397. The UK's Peregrine Falcon is the fastest bird in the world. What is its top speed when diving?
A) 60 mph
B) 99 mph
C) 150 mph
D) Over 200 mph

Section 8: British Art & Literature

398. Who wrote "Pride and Prejudice"?
A) Emily Brontë
B) Jane Austen
C) Charles Dickens
D) George Eliot

399. Which artist is known for his paintings of the industrial revolution, including "The Fighting Temeraire"?
A) John Constable
B) Francis Bacon
C) Thomas Gainsborough
D) J.M.W. Turner

400. "To be, or not to be" is a famous line from which Shakespeare play?
A) Othello
B) King Lear
C) Macbeth
D) Hamlet

401. Who is the author of "Middlemarch"?
A) Jane Austen
B) George Eliot
C) Mary Shelley
D) Virginia Woolf

402. What movement is William Wordsworth associated with?
A) Romanticism
B) Modernism
C) The Enlightenment
D) The Renaissance

403. Which poet wrote "Do not go gentle into that good night"?
A) W.B. Yeats
B) Philip Larkin
C) T.S. Eliot
D) Dylan Thomas

404. Who painted "Ophelia"?
A) John Everett Millais
B) Dante Gabriel Rossetti
C) William Holman Hunt
D) Ford Madox Brown

405. "1984" and "Animal Farm" were written by which author?
A) Aldous Huxley
B) George Orwell
C) Graham Greene
D) Evelyn Waugh

406. The Tate is a network of four art museums; which city are they all located in?
A) London
B) Manchester
C) Liverpool
D) Bristol

407. Who is the main character in Charles Dickens's "David Copperfield"?
A) Ebenezer Scrooge
B) Oliver Twist
C) David Copperfield
D) Pip

408. Which English author wrote "The Hobbit" and "The Lord of the Rings"?
A) J.R.R. Tolkien
B) C.S. Lewis
C) J.K. Rowling
D) Terry Pratchett

409. "The Lady of Shalott" is a painting by which Pre-Raphaelite artist?
A) John William Waterhouse
B) Edward Burne-Jones
C) William Morris
D) John Everett Millais

410. "The Rime of the Ancient Mariner" is a poem by:
A) Lord Byron
B) Percy Bysshe Shelley
C) John Keats
D) Samuel Taylor Coleridge

411. Which novel by Jane Austen centers around the character Elizabeth Bennet?
A) Emma
B) Sense and Sensibility
C) Persuasion
D) Pride and Prejudice

412. The Bloomsbury Group included which famous author?
A) Charles Dickens
B) Samuel Beckett
C) Virginia Woolf
D) Thomas Hardy

413. Who created the enigmatic painting "The Ambassadors," which features a distorted skull?
A) Hans Holbein the Younger
B) Anthony van Dyck
C) Thomas Gainsborough
D) Joshua Reynolds

414. The fictional detective Sherlock Holmes was created by:
A) Agatha Christie
B) Arthur Conan Doyle
C) G.K. Chesterton
D) P.D. James

415. Who wrote the Gothic novel "Frankenstein"?
A) Bram Stoker
B) Daphne du Maurier
C) Ann Radcliffe
D) Mary Shelley

416. Which British poet laureate wrote "The Charge of the Light Brigade"?
A) Robert Southey
B) William Wordsworth
C) Alfred, Lord Tennyson
D) Ted Hughes

417. "Gulliver's Travels" was written by:
A) Daniel Defoe
B) Jonathan Swift
C) Samuel Richardson
D) Henry Fielding

418. "Childe Harold's Pilgrimage" is a long narrative poem by:
A) William Blake
B) Samuel Taylor Coleridge
C) Lord Byron
D) John Milton

419. "The Hay Wain" is a painting by which British artist?
A) J.M.W. Turner
B) John Constable
C) Thomas Gainsborough
D) Henry Moore

420. Who wrote "The Canterbury Tales"?
A) Geoffrey Chaucer
B) William Shakespeare
C) John Milton
D) Thomas Malory

421. "Mrs. Dalloway" is a novel by:
A) D.H. Lawrence
B) E.M. Forster
C) Virginia Woolf
D) Iris Murdoch

422. Which of the following characters is not a creation of Charles Dickens?
A) Uriah Heep
B) Jay Gatsby
C) Fagin
D) Miss Havisham

423. "The Importance of Being Earnest" is a play by:
A) Oscar Wilde
B) George Bernard Shaw
C) Harold Pinter
D) Tom Stoppard

424. "Brighton Rock" is a novel by which British author?
A) Ian Fleming
B) Kingsley Amis
C) Graham Greene
D) Anthony Burgess

425. The sculpture "The Physical Energy" in London's Kensington Gardens was created by:
A) Henry Moore
B) Antony Gormley
C) Barbara Hepworth
D) George Frederick Watts

426. The "Tudor Rose" symbol was famously used in the portraits of which monarch?
A) Henry VII
B) Elizabeth I
C) Mary I
D) Henry VIII

427. Which artist is famous for his "English Landscape Series"?
A) David Hockney
B) Lucian Freud
C) Peter Lanyon
D) Paul Nash

428. "Under Milk Wood" is a radio play by which Welsh writer?
A) R.S. Thomas
B) Dylan Thomas
C) Seamus Heaney
D) Ted Hughes

429. Which novel features the fictional estate of Pemberley?
A) Jane Eyre
B) Wuthering Heights
C) Pride and Prejudice
D) Mansfield Park

430. "A Vision of the Last Judgment" is a painting by which British artist?
A) William Blake
B) John Martin
C) Francis Danby
D) J.M.W. Turner

431. Who is the author of "Brideshead Revisited"?
A) Evelyn Waugh
B) Graham Greene
C) Somerset Maugham
D) Anthony Powell

432. The "Angel of the North" is a contemporary sculpture by:
A) Damien Hirst
B) Antony Gormley
C) Anish Kapoor
D) Rachel Whiteread

433. "Lines Composed a Few Miles Above Tintern Abbey" is written by which poet?
A) William Wordsworth
B) Samuel Taylor Coleridge
C) John Keats
D) Percy Bysshe Shelley

434. Who is the author of "A Brief History of Time"?
A) Stephen Hawking
B) Richard Dawkins
C) Christopher Hitchens
D) Peter Higgs

435. What is the subtitle of Mary Shelley's "Frankenstein"?
A) The Modern Prometheus
B) The New Adam
C) The Gothic Monster
D) The Tale of Terror

436. Who was the British Poet Laureate from 1999 to 2009?
A) Ted Hughes
B) Carol Ann Duffy
C) Andrew Motion
D) Seamus Heaney

437. Which artist is known for the iconic album cover of The Beatles' "Sgt. Pepper's Lonely Hearts Club Band"?
A) Peter Blake
B) Damien Hirst
C) Banksy
D) David Hockney

438. What is the name of the main character in Samuel Richardson's novel "Pamela"?
A) Pamela Andrews
B) Clarissa Harlowe
C) Sophia Western
D) Moll Flanders

439. Which Romantic poet penned the lines "Beauty is truth, truth beauty"?
A) Lord Byron
B) Percy Bysshe Shelley
C) John Keats
D) William Wordsworth

440. Who wrote the play "Waiting for Godot"?
A) Harold Pinter
B) Tom Stoppard
C) Edward Albee
D) Samuel Beckett

441. "The Fighting Temeraire" was painted by which artist?
A) Thomas Gainsborough
B) Joshua Reynolds
C) John Constable
D) J.M.W. Turner

442. Which city is the setting for Charles Dickens' novel "Bleak House"?
A) Manchester
B) London
C) Liverpool
D) Edinburgh

443. The Victoria and Albert Museum is located in which UK city?
A) London
B) Edinburgh
C) Manchester
D) Birmingham

444. Which novel by Jane Austen features the character Mr. Knightley?
A) Pride and Prejudice
B) Emma
C) Sense and Sensibility
D) Mansfield Park

445. The "Ashes" series in cricket is traditionally played between England and which other country?
A) New Zealand
B) South Africa
C) India
D) Australia

446. Tracey Emin is a prominent figure in which British art movement?
A) The Pre-Raphaelites
B) The YBAs (Young British Artists)
C) The Bloomsbury Group
D) The Vorticists

447. What is the main theme of George Orwell's novel "1984"?
A) The importance of nature
B) The tragedy of war
C) The class struggle
D) The perils of totalitarianism

448. Which British playwright wrote "The Importance of Being Earnest"?
A) Noël Coward
B) George Bernard Shaw
C) Oscar Wilde
D) Tennessee Williams

449. Who painted "The Hay Wain"?
A) John Constable
B) J.M.W. Turner
C) Thomas Gainsborough
D) Henry Moore

450. "Wuthering Heights" was the only novel written by which author?
A) Charlotte Brontë
B) Emily Brontë
C) Anne Brontë
D) Jane Austen

Section 9: British Landmarks & Monuments

451. What is the name of the prehistoric monument located in Wiltshire, England?
A) Buckingham Palace
B) The Gherkin
C) Stonehenge
D) Big Ben

452. Which city is home to the historic Tower of London?
A) Manchester
B) London
C) Liverpool
D) Bristol

453. The Roman Baths can be found in which British city?
A) Bath
B) Edinburgh
C) Cardiff
D) York

454. Which landmark is a large Ferris wheel on the South Bank of the River Thames in London?
A) The London Eye
B) The Shard
C) The London Bridge
D) The Monument

455. The Shard is found in which city?
A) Glasgow
B) Manchester
C) Birmingham
D) London

456. Hadrian's Wall was built by the Romans to protect their colony from tribes from where?
A) Scotland
B) Wales
C) Ireland
D) Scandinavia

457. The British Museum is located in which area of London?
A) Soho
B) Covent Garden
C) Chelsea
D) Bloomsbury

458. Edinburgh Castle is built upon which extinct volcanic feature?
A) Arthur's Seat
B) Castle Rock
C) Calton Hill
D) Salisbury Crags

459. What is the official residence of the monarch of the United Kingdom in London?
A) Windsor Castle
B) Kensington Palace
C) St. James's Palace
D) Buckingham Palace

460. Windsor Castle is located in which English county?
A) Kent
B) Berkshire
C) Essex
D) Surrey

461. What is the main residence of the Duke and Duchess of Cambridge?
A) Clarence House
B) Balmoral Castle
C) Kensington Palace
D) Sandringham House

462. The Angel of the North statue is located near which city?
A) Newcastle
B) Leeds
C) Manchester
D) Bristol

463. The prehistoric site, Avebury, is known for what?
A) Its cathedral
B) Its stone circle
C) Its Roman fort
D) Its Viking ruins

464. The Beatles Story museum can be found in which city?
A) Manchester
B) Liverpool
C) London
D) Birmingham

465. The National Wallace Monument celebrates which Scottish hero?
A) Robert the Bruce
B) William Wallace
C) Rob Roy MacGregor
D) James Douglas

466. Which landmark is a ceremonial avenue in London, connecting Trafalgar Square to Buckingham Palace?
A) Fleet Street
B) Downing Street
C) The Strand
D) The Mall

467. Cardiff Castle is located in which UK country?
A) Scotland
B) England
C) Wales
D) Northern Ireland

468. The Clifton Suspension Bridge spans which river?
A) River Thames
B) River Severn
C) River Avon
D) River Trent

469. The Victoria and Albert Museum is found in which part of London?
A) South Kensington
B) East End
C) West End
D) North London

470. Blenheim Palace was the birthplace of which famous British figure?
A) Queen Victoria
B) Winston Churchill
C) William Shakespeare
D) Charles Darwin

471. The Giant's Causeway is located in which part of the United Kingdom?
A) Wales
B) Scotland
C) Northern Ireland
D) England

472. The Battle of Britain Memorial Flight is based at which RAF station?
A) RAF Waddington
B) RAF Lakenheath
C) RAF Brize Norton
D) RAF Coningsby

473. Which city is home to the historic ship, the HMS Victory?
A) Portsmouth
B) Plymouth
C) Southampton
D) Bristol

474. The Royal Pavilion is a distinctive building located in which seaside resort?
A) Blackpool
B) Brighton
C) Bournemouth
D) Torquay

475. The Millennium Stadium, known for hosting national sports events, is found in which city?
A) Cardiff
B) Edinburgh
C) London
D) Belfast

476. The Kelpies are a landmark featuring two horse-head sculptures located in which country?
A) Northern Ireland
B) Wales
C) England
D) Scotland

477. Which landmark in Cornwall is a unique botanical project consisting of biodomes?
A) The Lost Gardens of Heligan
B) Kew Gardens
C) The Eden Project
D) The Royal Botanic Gardens

478. What is the name of the official London residence of the Archbishop of Canterbury?
A) Lambeth Palace
B) Westminster Abbey
C) St. Paul's Cathedral
D) Canterbury Cathedral

479. The Jorvik Viking Centre is located in which city?
A) Newcastle
B) York
C) Norwich
D) Leicester

480. Which castle is associated with the legend of King Arthur and his knights?
A) Leeds Castle
B) Dover Castle
C) Tintagel Castle
D) Warwick Castle

481. The Beatrix Potter Gallery is located in which National Park?
A) Peak District
B) Lake District
C) Snowdonia
D) Dartmoor

482. The Cutty Sark, a historic sailing ship, is preserved in which part of London?
A) Greenwich
B) Docklands
C) Chelsea
D) Southwark

483. The Churchill War Rooms can be found underneath which London landmark?
A) The Houses of Parliament
B) The Imperial War Museum
C) The British Museum
D) Whitehall

484. Which is the oldest university in England?
A) University of Cambridge
B) University of Oxford
C) University of London
D) University of Manchester

485. The Imperial War Museum was originally established in which London park?
A) Hyde Park
B) Richmond Park
C) Regent's Park
D) Crystal Palace Park

486. The National Railway Museum is located in which city?
A) Manchester
B) Birmingham
C) Sheffield
D) York

487. The Royal Yacht Britannia is now permanently moored as a museum ship in which city?
A) Glasgow
B) Bristol
C) Liverpool
D) Edinburgh

488. The Cerne Abbas Giant is a hill figure located in which English county?
A) Cornwall
B) Dorset
C) Somerset
D) Wiltshire

489. Which of these landmarks is a UNESCO World Heritage Site located in Durham?
A) Durham Cathedral
B) The Roman Baths
C) The Tower of London
D) Hadrian's Wall

490. The Uffington White Horse is a prehistoric hill figure located in which English county?
A) Oxfordshire
B) Gloucestershire
C) Northumberland
D) Berkshire

491. The Severn Bridge connects England with which other UK country?
A) Scotland
B) Wales
C) Northern Ireland
D) Isle of Man

492. Which British monarch is associated with the construction of the lavish Hampton Court Palace?
A) Queen Elizabeth I
B) King Henry VIII
C) King James I
D) Queen Victoria

493. What year was the Tower of London built?
A) 1066
B) 1078
C) 1346
D) 1534

494. Which landmark is at the heart of Trafalgar Square?
A) Nelson's Column
B) The Cenotaph
C) Marble Arch
D) The Shard

495. Where in London can you find the Rosetta Stone?
A) The Tate Modern
B) The National Gallery
C) The Victoria and Albert Museum
D) The British Museum

496. Which city is the Minster Cathedral located in?
A) York
B) Canterbury
C) Durham
D) Winchester

497. In which city is the UK's oldest public museum, the Ashmolean Museum, located?
A) Oxford
B) Cambridge
C) London
D) Edinburgh

498. What is the name of the palace located in West London?
A) St. James's Palace
B) Kensington Palace
C) Hampton Court Palace
D) Buckingham Palace

499. Where would you find the historic ship, the HMS Belfast?
A) River Clyde
B) River Tyne
C) River Thames
D) River Severn

500. What is the name of the famous circle of standing stones in the English county of Wiltshire?
A) Avebury
B) Callanish Stones
C) Stonehenge
D) Castlerigg

501. What is the main building on Edinburgh's Royal Mile?
A) Holyrood Palace
B) Edinburgh Castle
C) St Giles' Cathedral
D) The Scottish Parliament Building

502. Which of these landmarks is a famous prehistoric monument in Shropshire?
A) The Uffington White Horse
B) The Cerne Abbas Giant
C) The Iron Bridge
D) Old Sarum

503. What is the name of the large bell within the clock tower at the north end of the Palace of Westminster?
A) Big Albert
B) Big Ben
C) Big William
D) Big Charles

504. The Kelpies, two horse-head sculptures, are located near which Scottish town?
A) Falkirk
B) Glasgow
C) Stirling
D) Edinburgh

505. Blenheim Palace is the birthplace of which historical figure?
A) Queen Elizabeth I
B) Sir Winston Churchill
C) William Shakespeare
D) Isaac Newton

506. Which castle is the official residence of the Queen when she is in Scotland?
A) Edinburgh Castle
B) Stirling Castle
C) Balmoral Castle
D) Holyrood Palace

507. Where in London is the Cenotaph located?
A) Trafalgar Square
B) Parliament Square
C) Whitehall
D) Piccadilly Circus

508. Which bridge in London opens in the middle to allow ships to pass through?
A) London Bridge
B) Tower Bridge
C) Westminster Bridge
D) Millennium Bridge

509. The Giant's Causeway is located in which part of the United Kingdom?
A) Scotland
B) Wales
C) Northern Ireland
D) England

510. In which English city would you find the John Rylands Library?
A) Manchester
B) Liverpool
C) Leeds
D) Birmingham

511. Where in England would you find the historical monument, Hadrian's Wall?
A) Along the border with Scotland
B) In Cornwall
C) In Kent
D) In the Midlands

Section 10: Famous Brits

512. Who is known as the "Father of the National Parks" in Britain?
A) John Muir
B) William Wordsworth
C) Octavia Hill
D) Julian Glover

513. Which British author wrote the novel "1984"?
A) George Orwell
B) Aldous Huxley
C) Graham Greene
D) Ian Fleming

514. Who was the first female Prime Minister of the United Kingdom?
A) Theresa May
B) Margaret Thatcher
C) Indira Gandhi
D) Angela Merkel

515. Which British scientist is credited with the discovery of penicillin?
A) Edward Jenner
B) Alexander Fleming
C) Isaac Newton
D) Charles Darwin

516. Who was the British monarch during the Victorian era?
A) Queen Elizabeth II
B) Queen Mary
C) King Edward VII
D) Queen Victoria

517. Which British band is known for the album "Sgt. Pepper's Lonely Hearts Club Band"?
A) The Who
B) Pink Floyd
C) The Rolling Stones
D) The Beatles

518. Who is the British theoretical physicist who wrote "A Brief History of Time"?
A) Stephen Hawking
B) Roger Penrose
C) Paul Dirac
D) Brian Cox

519. Who was the English poet who wrote "The Canterbury Tales"?
A) William Shakespeare
B) Geoffrey Chaucer
C) John Milton
D) Thomas Hardy

520. Which British actor is known for portraying James Bond in "Casino Royale" and "Skyfall"?
A) Sean Connery
B) Roger Moore
C) Pierce Brosnan
D) Daniel Craig

521. Who is the English playwright whose works include "Hamlet" and "Romeo and Juliet"?
A) Christopher Marlowe
B) William Shakespeare
C) Ben Jonson
D) John Webster

522. What British nurse became known as "The Lady with the Lamp" during the Crimean War?
A) Florence Nightingale
B) Mary Seacole
C) Edith Cavell
D) Clara Barton

523. Which British naturalist developed the theory of natural selection?
A) Alfred Russel Wallace
B) James Watson
C) Gregor Mendel
D) Charles Darwin

524. Who is the British graffiti artist with an undisclosed identity, known for the artwork "Girl With Balloon"?
A) Banksy
B) Damien Hirst
C) Tracey Emin
D) Shepard Fairey

525. Which British singer is known for the hit song "Someone Like You"?
A) Adele
B) Amy Winehouse
C) Ed Sheeran
D) Sam Smith

526. Who was the British Prime Minister who signed the Munich Agreement in 1938?
A) Winston Churchill
B) Neville Chamberlain
C) Clement Attlee
D) Anthony Eden

527. Which British author created the fictional detective Sherlock Holmes?
A) Charles Dickens
B) Agatha Christie
C) Arthur Conan Doyle
D) P.D. James

528. Who was the first female Briton to win a Nobel Prize?
A) Rosalind Franklin
B) Dorothy Hodgkin
C) Ada Lovelace
D) Marie Curie

529. Which British fashion designer is known for introducing the miniskirt in the 1960s?
A) Vivienne Westwood
B) Alexander McQueen
C) Mary Quant
D) Stella McCartney

530. Who is the famous British Formula 1 racing driver who has won multiple world championships?
A) Nigel Mansell
B) Jenson Button
C) James Hunt
D) Lewis Hamilton

531. Which English scientist is known for his laws of motion and gravity?
A) Michael Faraday
B) Stephen Hawking
C) Isaac Newton
D) Ernest Rutherford

532. Who was the first woman to be elected as a Member of Parliament (MP) in Britain?
A) Nancy Astor
B) Margaret Bondfield
C) Barbara Castle
D) Theresa May

533. Which British musician is nicknamed the "Rocket Man" after one of his hit songs?
A) Mick Jagger
B) David Bowie
C) Elton John
D) Rod Stewart

534. Who is the renowned British cosmologist who co-authored "The Large Scale Structure of Space-Time"?
A) Fred Hoyle
B) Martin Rees
C) Stephen Hawking
D) Roger Penrose

535. Which British nurse was known for her pioneering work in hand hygiene and aseptic techniques?
A) Agnes Hunt
B) Florence Nightingale
C) Mary Seacole
D) Elizabeth Garrett Anderson

536. Who was the first Briton to win the Tour de France?
A) Chris Froome
B) Geraint Thomas
C) Bradley Wiggins
D) Mark Cavendish

537. Which famous British author wrote "Pride and Prejudice"?
A) Charlotte Brontë
B) Mary Shelley
C) Emily Brontë
D) Jane Austen

538. Who is the British politician and leader known for his "Iron Curtain" speech?
A) Neville Chamberlain
B) Winston Churchill
C) Tony Blair
D) Harold Macmillan

539. Which British composer is known for his works such as "The Enigma Variations" and "Pomp and Circumstance"?
A) Benjamin Britten
B) Edward Elgar
C) Ralph Vaughan Williams
D) George Frideric Handel

540. Who was the female British monarch who reigned for 63 years and 7 months?
A) Queen Elizabeth I
B) Queen Elizabeth II
C) Queen Anne
D) Queen Victoria

541. Which British author wrote "The Lord of the Rings" and "The Hobbit"?
A) C.S. Lewis
B) J.K. Rowling
C) J.R.R. Tolkien
D) George R.R. Martin

542. What British physicist and mathematician is credited with the invention of calculus alongside Leibniz?
A) Michael Faraday
B) Isaac Newton
C) James Clerk Maxwell
D) Paul Dirac

543. Who is the famous British explorer who led three voyages to the Pacific Ocean, mapping many areas and recording several islands and coastlines on European maps for the first time?
A) Francis Drake
B) Walter Raleigh
C) James Cook
D) John Cabot

544. Which British filmmaker is known for directing "Psycho" and "The Birds"?
A) Alfred Hitchcock
B) Ridley Scott
C) Christopher Nolan
D) David Lean

545. Who is the British actress known for playing Hermione Granger in the "Harry Potter" film series?
A) Kate Winslet
B) Keira Knightley
C) Emma Thompson
D) Emma Watson

546. Which British physicist shared the Nobel Prize in Physics with his son for their work on the structure of the atom?
A) J.J. Thomson
B) Ernest Rutherford
C) James Chadwick
D) William Henry Bragg

547. Which British actor starred as the titular character in the "Borat" films?
A) Ricky Gervais
B) Russell Brand
C) Sacha Baron Cohen
D) Rowan Atkinson

548. Who is the British monarch responsible for the establishment of the Church of England?
A) Henry VII
B) Elizabeth I
C) James I
D) Henry VIII

549. Which British prime minister was awarded the Nobel Prize in Literature?
A) Harold Wilson
B) Winston Churchill
C) Tony Blair
D) Margaret Thatcher

550. Who is the British computer scientist credited with inventing the World Wide Web?
A) Alan Turing
B) Tim Berners-Lee
C) Charles Babbage
D) Stephen Hawking

551. Which British actress won an Academy Award for her role in "The Queen"?
A) Judi Dench
B) Helen Mirren
C) Kate Winslet
D) Emma Thompson

552. Who is the famous British street artist whose distinctive stenciled artworks have appeared around the world?
A) Banksy
B) Damien Hirst
C) Tracey Emin
D) David Hockney

553. Which British explorer is best known for his three voyages to Antarctica in the early 20th century?
A) Robert Falcon Scott
B) Ernest Shackleton
C) John Franklin
D) Francis Drake

554. Who was the legendary British leader who is said to have defended Britain against Saxon invaders in the late 5th and early 6th centuries?
A) King Alfred the Great
B) William the Conqueror
C) King Arthur
D) Richard the Lionheart

555. Which British actor is known for his role as Captain Jack Sparrow in the "Pirates of the Caribbean" series?
A) Ian McKellen
B) Daniel Day-Lewis
C) Johnny Depp
D) Orlando Bloom

556. Which British author created the James Bond series of spy novels?
A) Ian Fleming
B) John le Carré
C) Graham Greene
D) Arthur Conan Doyle

557. Who was the longest-reigning male monarch in British history before being surpassed by Queen Elizabeth II?
A) King George III
B) King Henry VIII
C) King Edward III
D) King James VI and I

558. Which British musician was the lead singer of the rock band Queen?
A) Rod Stewart
B) Freddie Mercury
C) David Bowie
D) Mick Jagger

559. Who was the British abolitionist and social reformer known for his role in the movement to abolish the slave trade?
A) Thomas Clarkson
B) William Wilberforce
C) Granville Sharp
D) Olaudah Equiano

560. Which British scientist won a Nobel Prize for his work on the discovery of the structure of DNA?
A) Maurice Wilkins
B) Rosalind Franklin
C) Francis Crick
D) James Watson

561. What British actor is known for his portrayal of the title character in "The Theory of Everything"?
A) Eddie Redmayne
B) Benedict Cumberbatch
C) Tom Hiddleston
D) Gary Oldman

Section 11: British TV & Film

562. Who plays the main character in the British TV series "Sherlock"?
A) Martin Freeman
B) Benedict Cumberbatch
C) Tom Hiddleston
D) Idris Elba

563. What is the name of the fictional town in "The Office" (UK)?
A) Wernham
B) Slough
C) Norwich
D) Reading

564. Which of these is a long-running British soap opera?
A) Emmerdale
B) The Bold and the Beautiful
C) Days of Our Lives
D) The Young and the Restless

565. Who wrote the novel that the TV series "Poldark" is based on?
A) Agatha Christie
B) Winston Graham
C) J.K. Rowling
D) Jane Austen

566. Which actor played the Ninth Doctor in "Doctor Who"?
A) David Tennant
B) Matt Smith
C) Christopher Eccleston
D) Peter Capaldi

567. What is the primary setting of the TV series "Downton Abbey"?
A) A hospital
B) A school
C) A hotel
D) A country estate

568. In "The Crown," who plays Queen Elizabeth II in the first two seasons?
A) Olivia Colman
B) Claire Foy
C) Helen Mirren
D) Judi Dench

569. What is the name of the main character in "Fleabag"?
A) Claire
B) Sarah
C) Louise
D) Fleabag (She is never given a proper name)

570. Which British city is the crime drama series "Peaky Blinders" set in?
A) Manchester
B) Liverpool
C) Birmingham
D) London

571. Who directed the film "Trainspotting"?
A) Guy Ritchie
B) Danny Boyle
C) Ridley Scott
D) Christopher Nolan

572. In which decade is the TV series "The Crown" initially set?
A) 1940s
B) 1950s
C) 1960s
D) 1970s

573. What is the profession of the main characters in "Absolutely Fabulous"?
A) Public Relations
B) Lawyers
C) Doctors
D) Police Officers

574. What is the name of the character played by Michaela Coel in "Chewing Gum"?
A) Tracey
B) Candice
C) Connie
D) Karly

575. "The Great British Bake Off" is a competition about what?
A) Singing
B) Dancing
C) Baking
D) Acting

576. Which actor plays the title character in the film "Bridget Jones's Diary"?
A) Kate Winslet
B) Emma Thompson
C) Keira Knightley
D) Renée Zellweger

577. In "Blackadder Goes Forth," what is the main setting?
A) The Renaissance
B) The Roman Empire
C) The Middle Ages
D) World War I

578. What is the main theme of the TV series "The IT Crowd"?
A) A group of friends living together
B) Doctors in a hospital
C) Lawyers in a corporate firm
D) The staff of an IT support team

579. Who starred as the main character in the film "The King's Speech"?
A) Geoffrey Rush
B) Hugh Grant
C) Colin Firth
D) Michael Gambon

580. The British TV series "Skins" mainly deals with what?
A) Spies and espionage
B) Teenagers and their lives
C) Historical drama
D) Medical professionals

581. In "Love Actually," how is the new Prime Minister related to one of the other main characters?
A) Brother
B) Father
C) Uncle
D) No relation

582. Which actor portrayed Mr. Bean?
A) Stephen Fry
B) Hugh Laurie
C) Rowan Atkinson
D) John Cleese

583. What is the profession of the protagonist in the TV series "Broadchurch"?
A) Journalist
B) Police Detective
C) Teacher
D) Doctor

584. In "The Vicar of Dibley," what is the vicar's name?
A) Geraldine
B) Susan
C) Julie
D) Margaret

585. What was the profession of the main character in "The Full Monty" before they become strippers?
A) Steelworkers
B) Miners
C) Fishermen
D) Farmers

586. Which of these series is a spin-off from "Doctor Who"?
A) Torchwood
B) Red Dwarf
C) The Avengers
D) Black Mirror

587. Who is the star of the British TV series "Luther"?
A) Chiwetel Ejiofor
B) Idris Elba
C) David Harewood
D) Morgan Freeman

588. What is the name of the alien race in "Doctor Who" that looks like pepper pots?
A) The Silurians
B) The Cybermen
C) The Daleks
D) The Sontarans

589. Who directed "Slumdog Millionaire"?
A) Stephen Daldry
B) Mike Leigh
C) Danny Boyle
D) Sam Mendes

590. Which British historical figure is the central character in "The Favourite"?
A) Queen Elizabeth I
B) Queen Victoria
C) Queen Anne
D) Mary, Queen of Scots

591. What is the main character's occupation in "Prime Suspect"?
A) A teacher
B) A journalist
C) A police detective
D) A lawyer

592. "Notting Hill" features a love story between a bookshop owner and:
A) A chef
B) A movie star
C) A musician
D) A model

593. In "The Inbetweeners," where do the four friends go on holiday?
A) Malia
B) Ibiza
C) Crete
D) Magaluf

594. Which TV series is based on a set of novels by Bernard Cornwell?
A) The Last Kingdom
B) Game of Thrones
C) Outlander
D) Poldark

595. Who played James Bond in "Casino Royale" (2006)?
A) Sean Connery
B) Roger Moore
C) Pierce Brosnan
D) Daniel Craig

596. What is the name of the pub in "Shaun of the Dead"?
A) The World's End
B) The Winchester
C) The Golden Lion
D) The King's Head

597. In which TV show does the character "Hyacinth Bucket" appear?
A) Keeping Up Appearances
B) As Time Goes By
C) The Good Life
D) Are You Being Served?

598. What is the name of the fictional estate in "Gosford Park"?
A) Blythe Manor
B) Downton Abbey
C) Gosford Park
D) Wrotham Park

599. Who created the TV series "Line of Duty"?
A) Julian Fellowes
B) Steven Knight
C) Jed Mercurio
D) Russell T Davies

600. Who created the British TV series "Black Mirror"?
A) Charlie Brooker
B) Russell T. Davies
C) Steven Moffat
D) Graham Linehan

601. Which actor played the title role in the British TV series "Cracker"?
A) Sean Bean
B) Robbie Coltrane
C) Robert Carlyle
D) Hugh Laurie

602. What is the name of the fictional suburb in "The Royle Family"?
A) Prestwich
B) Chatsworth
C) Peckham
D) Runcorn

603. Who played Queen Elizabeth I in the film "Elizabeth"?
A) Cate Blanchett
B) Helen Mirren
C) Judi Dench
D) Kate Winslet

604. In "The IT Crowd," what is the name of the company that the characters work for?
A) Reynholm Industries
B) Wernham Hogg
C) Initech
D) Goliath Corporation

605. Who directed "Four Weddings and a Funeral"?
A) Richard Curtis
B) Mike Newell
C) Ken Loach
D) Danny Boyle

606. What was the name of the café in the sitcom "Open All Hours"?
A) Arkwright's
B) Granville's
C) Roy's Rolls
D) The Cutlers

607. What was the main setting of the TV series "Last of the Summer Wine"?
A) A pub
B) A community center
C) A village in Yorkshire
D) A London borough

608. Who played the lead role in the British drama series "Broadchurch"?
A) David Tennant
B) Martin Freeman
C) Benedict Cumberbatch
D) Matt Smith

609. In the film "Love Actually," who does the Prime Minister fall in love with?
A) His secretary
B) A journalist
C) His caterer
D) A schoolteacher

610. What is the name of the protagonist in "Absolutely Fabulous"?
A) Patsy
B) Edina
C) Saffron
D) Bubble

611. What is the primary job of the lead character in "Luther"?
A) Forensic psychologist
B) Detective Chief Inspector
C) Profiler
D) Criminal lawyer

612. Which of these characters is NOT from "The Inbetweeners"?
A) Jay
B) Simon
C) Neil
D) Vince

613. In "Keeping Up Appearances," what does Hyacinth Bucket insist her last name be pronounced as?
A) Bouquet
B) Bucké
C) Buckay
D) Bucket

614. What is the name of the main character in "The Vicar of Dibley"?
A) Geraldine Granger
B) Alice Tinker
C) Hugo Horton
D) David Horton

615. Which British actor plays the lead role in the "Harry Potter" film series?
A) Rupert Grint
B) Daniel Radcliffe
C) Tom Felton
D) Matthew Lewis

Section 12: British Music

616. What was the original name of the British band The Beatles?
A) The Who
B) Pink Floyd
C) The Beatles
D) Led Zeppelin

617. Amy Winehouse was primarily known for her unique voice in which genre of music?
A) Pop
B) R&B
C) Jazz
D) Hip-Hop

618. Which Oasis hit single begins with the lyric "Today is gonna be the day"?
A) Wonderwall
B) Champagne Supernova
C) Don't Look Back in Anger
D) Live Forever

619. Which British artist released the album "÷ (Divide)" in 2017?
A) Ed Sheeran
B) Adele
C) Sam Smith
D) James Bay

620. What is the real name of the iconic British musician known as Sting?
A) Gordon Sumner
B) David Evans
C) Richard Starkey
D) John Lydon

621. "Bohemian Rhapsody" is a hit song by which British band?
A) The Rolling Stones
B) Queen
C) The Kinks
D) The Clash

622. Adele made her debut with which album?
A) 19
B) 21
C) 25
D) 30

623. Which band is known for the hit "You Really Got Me"?
A) The Beatles
B) The Who
C) The Kinks
D) The Animals

624. Which artist is famous for the song "Shape of You"?
A) Robbie Williams
B) Ed Sheeran
C) Calvin Harris
D) Harry Styles

625. "Back to Black" and "Rehab" are songs by which British artist?
A) Duffy
B) Amy Winehouse
C) Lily Allen
D) Adele

626. Which British girl group had a member by the name of Ginger Spice?
A) All Saints
B) Spice Girls
C) Little Mix
D) Atomic Kitten

627. The song "Parklife" is associated with which British band?
A) Blur
B) Oasis
C) Pulp
D) The Verve

628. "Yellow" and "Fix You" are hits by which British band?
A) Coldplay
B) Radiohead
C) Keane
D) Muse

629. What was the title of Phil Collins' first solo album released in 1981?
A) But Seriously
B) No Jacket Required
C) Face Value
D) Both Sides

630. Which British singer became famous with the song "Your Song" in the early 1970s?
A) Rod Stewart
B) David Bowie
C) Elton John
D) Paul McCartney

631. "West End Girls" is a famous song by which duo?
A) Pet Shop Boys
B) Erasure
C) Eurythmics
D) Soft Cell

632. Which British musician is known for the hit single "Let Me Entertain You"?
A) Robbie Williams
B) George Michael
C) Sting
D) Mick Jagger

633. The album "Hunky Dory" includes the song "Life on Mars" and is by which artist?
A) The Beatles
B) Queen
C) David Bowie
D) Elton John

634. Who is the lead singer of the British rock band Led Zeppelin?
A) Freddie Mercury
B) Robert Plant
C) Roger Daltrey
D) David Gilmour

635. "Freed from Desire" was a hit for which British singer?
A) Dua Lipa
B) Gala
C) Jess Glynne
D) Rita Ora

636. Which English musician is known for his red-headed appearance and hit song "Angels"?
A) Ed Sheeran
B) Phil Collins
C) Elton John
D) Robbie Williams

637. Which British band is known for their album "(What's the Story) Morning Glory?"?
A) Blur
B) Oasis
C) The Stone Roses
D) Arctic Monkeys

638. "Rolling in the Deep" and "Someone Like You" are hits from which British artist's album "21"?
A) Leona Lewis
B) Adele
C) Amy Winehouse
D) Duffy

639. The Smiths were a seminal band in the 1980s with which frontman?
A) Morrissey
B) Johnny Marr
C) Robert Smith
D) Ian Curtis

640. Which band released the gothic rock album "Disintegration" in 1989?
A) The Cure
B) Joy Division
C) The Sisters of Mercy
D) Bauhaus

641. "Common People" is a well-known Britpop song by which band?
A) Blur
B) Pulp
C) Supergrass
D) Oasis

642. Which British-American band released the highly successful album "Rumours"?
A) Fleetwood Mac
B) The Rolling Stones
C) Pink Floyd
D) Eagles

643. "Firestarter" is a hit song by which British electronic group?
A) The Chemical Brothers
B) Fatboy Slim
C) The Prodigy
D) Orbital

644. Which British band was fronted by the singer Ian Brown?
A) The Stone Roses
B) The Charlatans
C) Blur
D) Oasis

645. "Iron Man" and "Paranoid" are famous tracks by which English rock band?
A) Judas Priest
B) Black Sabbath
C) Motorhead
D) Iron Maiden

646. Which band, formed in London in 1968, is considered one of the pioneers of heavy metal?
A) Deep Purple
B) Led Zeppelin
C) Black Sabbath
D) The Who

647. "Enjoy the Silence" is a hit from which British band?
A) Depeche Mode
B) New Order
C) The Cure
D) Duran Duran

648. What was the best-selling UK single of the 1970s, performed by a British-Swedish band?
A) "Mamma Mia" by ABBA
B) "Bohemian Rhapsody" by Queen
C) "Night Fever" by Bee Gees
D) "Dancing Queen" by ABBA

649. Which British artist sang "Tears Dry On Their Own"?
A) Adele
B) Duffy
C) Amy Winehouse
D) Joss Stone

650. "Rio" and "Hungry Like the Wolf" are songs by which new wave band?
A) The Smiths
B) The Clash
C) Duran Duran
D) The Police

651. Before achieving fame as a solo artist, Peter Gabriel was the original lead singer of which band?
A) Genesis
B) Yes
C) King Crimson
D) The Moody Blues

652. Which English rock band, formed in London in 1964, had a hit with "Paint It, Black"?
A) The Kinks
B) The Rolling Stones
C) The Who
D) The Yardbirds

653. "Can't Get You Out of My Head" was a global hit for which Australian-born singer, often associated with the UK music scene?
A) Natalie Imbruglia
B) Kylie Minogue
C) Sia
D) Iggy Azalea

654. "Stay With Me" is a song by which British singer and songwriter?
A) Ed Sheeran
B) Sam Smith
C) James Arthur
D) John Newman

655. Which band released the influential album "OK Computer" in 1997?
A) Blur
B) Oasis
C) Radiohead
D) Coldplay

656. Who released the song "Space Oddity" days before the Apollo 11 moon landing in 1969?
A) The Beatles
B) Elton John
C) David Bowie
D) Pink Floyd

657. Which band is known for their rock opera album "Tommy"?
A) The Beatles
B) Pink Floyd
C) The Who
D) Queen

658. What is the title of the debut studio album by the English indie rock band Arctic Monkeys?
A) AM
B) Favourite Worst Nightmare
C) Whatever People Say I Am, That's What I'm Not
D) Tranquility Base Hotel & Casino

659. Which British rock band was named after a sculpture in London that has the full name "The Angel of the North"?
A) Judas Priest
B) Iron Maiden
C) Def Leppard
D) Motörhead

660. Who had a 1980s hit with "Don't You Want Me"?
A) The Human League
B) The Eurythmics
C) Soft Cell
D) Depeche Mode

661. Which iconic British band was formed in London in 1970 by Freddie Mercury, Brian May, Roger Taylor, and John Deacon?
A) Queen
B) The Beatles
C) Led Zeppelin
D) The Rolling Stones

662. "Wannabe" was the debut single of which all-female British pop group?
A) Spice Girls
B) Girls Aloud
C) Little Mix
D) The Saturdays

663. "The Dark Side of the Moon" is an album by which British band?
A) The Who
B) Pink Floyd
C) Led Zeppelin
D) The Rolling Stones

664. Who had a hit in the 1980s with "Sweet Dreams (Are Made of This)"?
A) The Eurythmics
B) Wham!
C) Culture Club
D) Duran Duran

665. "Anarchy in the U.K." is a famous track by which British punk band?
A) The Clash
B) The Damned
C) Sex Pistols
D) Buzzcocks

Section 13: British Holidays & Celebrations

666. What is traditionally eaten on Shrove Tuesday in the UK?
A) Fish and chips
B) Pancakes
C) Roast beef
D) Pie and mash

667. Which saint's day is celebrated by the Welsh on March 1st?
A) St. David
B) St. Andrew
C) St. George
D) St. Patrick

668. What event is commemorated on Guy Fawkes Night?
A) The end of the English Civil War
B) The coronation of Queen Elizabeth II
C) The Gunpowder Plot of 1605
D) The Battle of Britain

669. On what date is St. George's Day celebrated?
A) April 23
B) March 17
C) November 30
D) January 25

670. Which flower is traditionally worn on Remembrance Day?
A) Rose
B) Daffodil
C) Poppy
D) Lily

671. What is Boxing Day?
A) A day dedicated to the sport of boxing
B) The day after Christmas Day
C) A bank holiday in August
D) The Queen's birthday

672. When is the traditional British holiday season known as the 'Twelve Days of Christmas'?
A) December 1-12
B) December 25 - January 5
C) December 24 - January 4
D) November 25 - December 6

673. Which British celebration is known for its association with fireworks?
A) Easter
B) May Day
C) Bonfire Night
D) Boxing Day

674. What is the traditional race that takes place on Pancake Day?
A) The Pancake Flip Race
B) The Great British Run
C) The Pancake Toss
D) The Pancake Day Race

675. Which city hosts the largest New Year's Eve celebration in Scotland, known as Hogmanay?
A) Glasgow
B) Dundee
C) Aberdeen
D) Edinburgh

676. On which date do the British celebrate Mother's Day, also known as Mothering Sunday?
A) The fourth Sunday in Lent
B) The second Sunday in May
C) March 8
D) The first Sunday in June

677. During which holiday might you encounter 'morris dancing' in England?
A) Halloween
B) Christmas
C) May Day
D) Easter

678. The Notting Hill Carnival is a celebration associated with which community?
A) Chinese
B) Caribbean
C) Indian
D) Polish

679. In the UK, what is celebrated on the second Saturday in June?
A) The Queen's actual birthday
B) The Queen's official birthday
C) Independence Day
D) Victory in Europe Day

680. What do children traditionally do on Halloween in the UK?
A) Carol singing
B) Bonfire jumping
C) Trick-or-treating
D) Maypole dancing

681. What is the name of the Sunday before Easter?
A) Good Friday
B) Easter Sunday
C) Palm Sunday
D) Maundy Thursday

682. What event does the Chelsea Flower Show celebrate?
A) Fashion
B) Literature
C) Horticulture
D) Music

683. Which of the following days is a bank holiday in the UK by tradition?
A) April Fool's Day
B) Boxing Day
C) Halloween
D) Valentine's Day

684. When is Burns Night celebrated?
A) January 25
B) February 14
C) March 17
D) November 5

685. What is the significance of the Trooping the Colour ceremony?
A) It celebrates the British Army's history
B) It honors the Queen's birthday
C) It marks the start of the parliamentary year
D) It commemorates the signing of the Magna Carta

686. What do people traditionally do on May Day in some English villages?
A) Light bonfires
B) Dance around the maypole
C) Throw tomatoes at each other
D) Fly kites

687. When do the British celebrate Father's Day?
A) The third Sunday in June
B) The third Sunday in May
C) April 1
D) The last Sunday of March

688. What is a pantomime associated with in Britain?
A) Christmas
B) Easter
C) Summer holidays
D) Halloween

689. The Summer Solstice is often celebrated at which ancient British site?
A) Hadrian's Wall
B) Tower of London
C) Stonehenge
D) Buckingham Palace

690. What fruit is traditionally associated with Wimbledon, the tennis championship held in London?
A) Apples
B) Strawberries
C) Oranges
D) Bananas

691. What is the significance of the Red Arrows flypast in the UK?
A) It is a display for New Year's Day.
B) It commemorates Remembrance Day.
C) It is a part of the Queen's official birthday celebrations.
D) It marks the end of the summer season.

692. Which festival involves rolling a wheel of cheese down a hill and chasing after it?
A) The Gloucestershire Cheese Rolling
B) The Cheddar Challenge
C) The Wensleydale Rush
D) The Stilton Sprint

693. When is the traditional British harvest festival usually celebrated?
A) Around the time of the Harvest Moon, close to the autumn equinox
B) In mid-summer
C) During Easter
D) At the beginning of spring

694. The Lord Mayor's Show is an annual event in which city?
A) Manchester
B) London
C) Bristol
D) Edinburgh

695. In Scotland, what name is given to New Year's Eve celebrations?
A) Beltane
B) Samhain
C) Hogmanay
D) Burns Night

Section 14: British Inventions

696. Who is credited with inventing the World Wide Web?
A) Alan Turing
B) Tim Berners-Lee
C) Alexander Graham Bell
D) Michael Faraday

697. The jet engine was invented by which British engineer?
A) Frank Whittle
B) Henry Royce
C) George Stephenson
D) James Watt

698. What year was the first successful photograph taken by British inventor Joseph Nicéphore Niépce?
A) 1765
B) 1826
C) 1876
D) 1901

699. The structure known as the "Iron Bridge" was the first arch bridge made of cast iron, but in which British county can it be found?
A) Cornwall
B) Shropshire
C) Surrey
D) Kent

700. Who invented the seed drill in 1701, revolutionizing agriculture?
A) Jethro Tull
B) Charles Babbage
C) Isaac Newton
D) Edward Jenner

701. The pneumatic tire was patented by which Scotsman in 1888?
A) John Boyd Dunlop
B) Robert William Thomson
C) James Dyson
D) Kirkpatrick Macmillan

702. The first programmable computer, the Colossus, was built to crack codes during which war?
A) World War I
B) World War II
C) The Cold War
D) The Korean War

703. Which British invention was key to the development of modern computers by storing and running programs?
A) The Steam Engine
B) The Spinning Jenny
C) The Analytical Engine
D) The Electric Motor

704. The iconic London Underground, the first subway system in the world, opened in what year?
A) 1753
B) 1863
C) 1899
D) 1905

705. Who is known for inventing the smallpox vaccine in 1796?
A) Edward Jenner
B) Alexander Fleming
C) Joseph Lister
D) Thomas Crapper

706. In what year was the reflecting telescope invented by Sir Isaac Newton?
A) 1668
B) 1705
C) 1759
D) 1801

707. The discovery of penicillin in 1928 is attributed to which British scientist?
A) Henry Moseley
B) Humphry Davy
C) Francis Crick
D) Alexander Fleming

708. The marine chronometer, a timepiece used for navigation at sea, was invented by which British clockmaker?
A) John Harrison
B) George Graham
C) Edward John Dent
D) Thomas Tompion

709. Which British inventor is credited with creating the first practical telephone?
A) Alexander Graham Bell
B) Charles Wheatstone
C) John Logie Baird
D) Thomas Edison

710. What British innovation, developed by George Cayley, greatly contributed to the modern field of aeronautics?
A) The Jet Engine
B) The Helicopter
C) The Aileron
D) The Parachute

711. Who was the British inventor of the police truncheon?
A) Sir Robert Peel
B) Henry Mayhew
C) William Ewart Gladstone
D) John Hobbins

712. The invention of the safety bicycle, with its rear-wheel chain drive, is often attributed to which British inventor?
A) James Starley
B) Harry John Lawson
C) Kirkpatrick Macmillan
D) John Kemp Starley

713. In which year did Michael Faraday create the first electric generator?
A) 1821
B) 1871
C) 1851
D) 1831

714. The waterproof material known as Mackintosh was invented by which Scotsman?
A) James Macintosh
B) John MacAdam
C) Charles Macintosh
D) Alexander MacMillan

715. In 1876, who patented the first practical telephone, although Alexander Graham Bell was the first to be awarded a patent for it?
A) Thomas Edison
B) John Logie Baird
C) Antonio Meucci
D) Elisha Gray

716. The invention of the modern steam locomotive is attributed to which British engineer?
A) Richard Trevithick
B) George Stephenson
C) James Watt
D) Matthew Boulton

717. The first successful chocolate bar was made by which British company?
A) Cadbury
B) Nestlé
C) Fry's
D) Terry's

718. The automatic kettle that switches itself off once water reaches boiling point was invented by which British engineer?
A) Peter Hobbs
B) Michael Faraday
C) John C. Taylor
D) James Dyson

719. In which year was the first professional police force, known as the Metropolitan Police Service, established in London?
A) 1750
B) 1829
C) 1875
D) 1901

720. The Christmas card is a British invention first introduced in what year?
A) 1611
B) 1743
C) 1843
D) 1894

721. The television, a device that would become a global commodity, was first successfully demonstrated by which British inventor?
A) John Logie Baird
B) Philo Farnsworth
C) Guglielmo Marconi
D) Nikola Tesla

722. Which British engineer and inventor is known for developing the first practical hovercraft?
A) Sir Christopher Cockerell
B) Sir Frank Whittle
C) Sir George Cayley
D) Sir Barnes Wallis

723. The modern-day ATM was first conceived by which British inventor?
A) James Goodfellow
B) John Shepherd-Barron
C) William Smith
D) David H. Jones

724. What is the name of the British inventor who pioneered the development of the modern electric vacuum cleaner?
A) Hubert Cecil Booth
B) James Dyson
C) Harry Booth
D) Freddie Hoover

725. The discovery of hydrogen by Henry Cavendish was announced in which year?
A) 1756
B) 1766
C) 1781
D) 1800

726. The game of association football (soccer) was first codified in which year in England?
A) 1815
B) 1848
C) 1863
D) 1901

727. Which British physician's work led to the development of the clinical thermometer?
A) Thomas Allbutt
B) Edward Jenner
C) Joseph Lister
D) John Snow

728. The lawnmower was invented by Edwin Beard Budding in which year?
A) 1750
B) 1830
C) 1899
D) 1925

729. Who is considered the inventor of the modern float glass process, revolutionizing the production of flat glass?
A) Alastair Pilkington
B) Henry Bessemer
C) James Dyson
D) Joseph Swan

730. The sandwich is named after the 4th Earl of Sandwich, but what was his actual name?
A) John Montagu
B) Thomas Sandwich
C) James Cook
D) William Rich

731. In 1895, who invented the first portable, "clockwork" film camera?
A) Robert W. Paul
B) John Logie Baird
C) William Friese-Greene
D) Charles Babbage

732. Who is credited with the invention of shorthand in 1602?
A) Sir Isaac Pitman
B) John Robert Gregg
C) Tim Berners-Lee
D) Samuel Taylor

733. The carbonated soft drink 'Schweppes' was developed by Jacob Schweppe, but where in Britain was the company founded?
A) London
B) Birmingham
C) Geneva
D) Bristol

734. The first successful electric telegraph was built by Sir Charles Wheatstone and Sir William Fothergill Cooke in which year?
A) 1837
B) 1844
C) 1861
D) 1876

735. Who invented the first practical dishwashing machine in the 1920s?
A) Josephine Cochrane
B) William Howard Livens
C) Alexander Graham Bell
D) James Dyson

736. Which British inventor is known for creating the bouncing bomb used in the WWII "Dambusters" raid?
A) Sir Barnes Wallis
B) Sir Frank Whittle
C) Sir Christopher Cockerell
D) Alan Turing

737. In which year was the first British patent issued for a locomotive steam engine?
A) 1698
B) 1804
C) 1825
D) 1876

738. Who patented the first practical typewriter and the QWERTY keyboard layout?
A) Christopher Latham Sholes
B) Henry Mill
C) Charles Thurber
D) Alexander Bain

739. The stereophonic sound was first demonstrated by Alan Blumlein in which year?
A) 1931
B) 1933
C) 1940
D) 1952

740. The Catseye, a device used to improve road safety, was invented by Percy Shaw in what year?
A) 1903
B) 1924
C) 1934
D) 1955

Section 15: British World Records

741. Who is the British author with the best-selling book series in history?
A) J.R.R. Tolkien
B) J.K. Rowling
C) Agatha Christie
D) Ian Fleming

742. Which British athlete holds the record for the fastest marathon in a full-body animal costume?
A) Paula Radcliffe
B) David Stone
C) Tom Harrison
D) Mo Farah

743. The record for the largest scone ever made was set in Britain. How much did it weigh?
A) 10 kilograms
B) 93 kilograms
C) 119 kilograms
D) 146 kilograms

744. What is the name of the British woman who holds the record for the longest space flight by a woman?
A) Helen Sharman
B) Sally Ride
C) Valentina Tereshkova
D) Peggy Whitson

745. Which British band holds the record for the most concerts performed in a year?
A) The Beatles
B) The Rolling Stones
C) Status Quo
D) One Direction

746. The world's fastest shed was built and driven by a Brit. How fast did it go to achieve the record?
A) 48 mph
B) 70.8 mph
C) 80.8 mph
D) 101.5 mph

747. The record for the largest gathering of people dressed as Sherlock Holmes was set in Britain. How many participants were there?
A) 113
B) 257
C) 443
D) 539

748. Who holds the record for the longest running TV weather presenter in the world?
A) Michael Fish
B) Ian McCaskill
C) Jim Hickey
D) Carol Kirkwood

749. The world's largest meat pie was cooked in Britain. How heavy was it?
A) 5,950 pounds
B) 2,290 pounds
C) 1,102 pounds
D) 10,540 pounds

750. Which British inventor holds the record for the most patents filed?
A) James Dyson
B) Trevor Baylis
C) Kane Kramer
D) Graham Bell

751. The largest collection of vacuum cleaners is held by a Brit. Approximately how many does he own?
A) More than 1000
B) More than 40
C) More than 5000
D) More than 300

752. A British cat holds the record for the longest jump by a cat. How far did it jump?
A) 6 feet (1.83 meters)
B) 7 feet (2.13 meters)
C) 9 feet (2.74 meters)
D) 12 feet (3.65 meters)

753. What record did British athlete Jonathan Edwards set in triple jump?
A) 18.29 meters
B) 17.77 meters
C) 18.97 meters
D) 18.43 meters

754. The world's fastest speedboat record was set by a British team. What was their speed?
A) 278.1 mph
B) 297.7 mph
C) 310.6 mph
D) 354.4 mph

755. The largest environmental charity walk in the world took place in the UK. How many walkers participated?
A) 12,500
B) 23,500
C) 33,000
D) 40,000

756. Which British individual holds the record for the deepest solo submersible dive?
A) Richard Branson
B) James Cameron
C) Victor Vescovo
D) Don Walsh

757. The largest rugby scrum was held in Britain with how many participants?
A) 1,198
B) 1,745
C) 2,586
D) 3,659

758. The world record for the fastest 100 meters in high heels is held by a Brit. What was her time?
A) 13.52 seconds
B) 14.531 seconds
C) 15.86 seconds
D) 17.03 seconds

759. Which British cyclist holds the record for the fastest circumnavigation by bicycle?
A) Sir Bradley Wiggins
B) Mark Beaumont
C) Chris Hoy
D) Geraint Thomas

760. The record for the oldest person to row across any ocean solo was set by a Brit at what age?
A) 66 years
B) 70 years
C) 72 years
D) 77 years

761. The world's longest-running soap opera is British. What is its name?
A) EastEnders
B) Coronation Street
C) Emmerdale
D) The Archers

762. Who was the youngest Brit to climb Mount Everest?
A) Rob Gauntlett
B) Bear Grylls
C) George Atkinson
D) Jake Meyer

763. Who holds the record for the longest serving TV newsreader in the world?
A) Trevor McDonald
B) Jon Snow
C) Angela Rippon
D) Huw Edwards

764. How long did it take for a British woman to set the record for the fastest solo journey to the South Pole?
A) 40 days
B) 50 days
C) 59 days
D) 70 days

765. Approximately many coins were used in creating the world's largest coin mosaic in Britain?
A) 247,000
B) 256,000
C) 300,000
D) 400,000

766. What is the record for the longest non-stop double-deck bus service in Britain?
A) From London to Edinburgh
B) From Glasgow to London
C) From Bristol to Aberdeen
D) From London to Gibraltar

767. How long is the largest commercially available hot dog sold in Britain?
A) 1 meter
B) 2 meters
C) 3 meters
D) 4 meters

768. Which symphony was played by a British orchestra in the world's longest symphony performance?
A) Beethoven's Ninth
B) Mahler's Third
C) Wagner's Ring Cycle
D) Shostakovich's Seventh

769. Who holds the record for the longest time spent in space by a Briton?
A) Tim Peake
B) Helen Sharman
C) Michael Foale
D) Piers Sellers

770. How tall was the tallest man ever from Britain?
   A) 8 ft 1 in
   B) 8 ft 4 in
   C) 9 ft 3 in
   D) 7 ft 7 in

Section 16: British Guess The Year

771. In which year was the Battle of Hastings fought?
A) 1066
B) 1077
C) 1088
D) 1099

772. In which year did Queen Elizabeth II ascend to the throne?
A) 1952
B) 1945
C) 1961
D) 1955

773. In which year was the Magna Carta signed?
A) 1199
B) 1215
C) 1250
D) 1301

774. When was the Great Fire of London?
A) 1686
B) 1676
C) 1666
D) 1656

775. When did the United Kingdom join the European Economic Community (EEC), which later became the European Union (EU)?
A) 1983
B) 1963
C) 1993
D) 1973

776. When was the Bank of England established?
A) 1649
B) 1706
C) 1724
D) 1694

777. In what year did the Titanic sink on its maiden voyage?
A) 1910
B) 1912
C) 1914
D) 1916

778. When did women over the age of 30 get the right to vote in Britain?
A) 1918
B) 1928
C) 1938
D) 1948

779. In which year was the Battle of Britain fought during World War II?
A) 1939
B) 1940
C) 1941
D) 1942

780. When did the Beatles release their influential album "Sgt. Pepper's Lonely Hearts Club Band"?
A) 1965
B) 1967
C) 1969
D) 1971

781. In what year was the London Underground, the world's first underground railway, opened?
A) 1863
B) 1873
C) 1883
D) 1893

782. When was the current London Bridge opened to traffic?
A) 1967
B) 1971
C) 1973
D) 1976

783. In which year was the "decimal day", the day on which the United Kingdom and Ireland decimalized their currencies?
A) 1961
B) 1971
C) 1981
D) 1991

784. When did the Channel Tunnel between the UK and France officially open?
A) 1984
B) 1994
C) 2004
D) 2014

785. When was the first Epsom Derby horse race held?
A) 1780
B) 1800
C) 1820
D) 1840

786. When did the "Swinging Sixties", a period of cultural revolution, reach its peak in London?
A) 1960
B) 1964
C) 1966
D) 1968

787. In what year was the "Great Exhibition" held in London, showcasing the wonders of industry and culture?
A) 1841
B) 1851
C) 1861
D) 1871

788. When was William Shakespeare born?
A) 1544
B) 1564
C) 1584
D) 1604

789. When did the British Broadcasting Corporation (BBC) begin regular television broadcasts?
A) 1956
B) 1946
C) 1936
D) 1926

790. In which year did the British Nationality Act create the status of "Citizen of the United Kingdom and Colonies"?
A) 1948
B) 1958
C) 1968
D) 1978

791. When did the "Winter of Discontent," a period of economic and social unrest, occur in the UK?
A) 1968
B) 1970
C) 1978
D) 1982

792. When was the "Glorious Revolution" in which William of Orange took the English throne from James II?
A) 1668
B) 1688
C) 1708
D) 1728

793. In which year did the "Falklands War" between the UK and Argentina take place?
A) 1980
B) 1982
C) 1984
D) 1986

794. When did the "Big Bang" deregulation of the financial markets occur in London?
A) 2006
B) 1976
C) 1996
D) 1986

795. In what year was the Stonehenge site officially added to the UNESCO list of World Heritage Sites?
A) 1992
B) 1982
C) 1989
D) 1986

796. When was the first Notting Hill Carnival, an event celebrating Caribbean culture in London?
A) 1959
B) 1964
C) 1969
D) 1974

797. When did the Great Smog of London take place, resulting in new clean air legislation?
A) 1952
B) 1956
C) 1960
D) 1964

798. When was the Anglo-Irish Agreement signed, aiming to help end the conflict in Northern Ireland?
A) 1981
B) 1985
C) 1989
D) 1993

799. When did Margaret Thatcher become the first female Prime Minister of the UK?
A) 1982
B) 1980
C) 1979
D) 1977

800. In which year was the London Eye officially opened to the public?
A) 1999
B) 2000
C) 2001
D) 2002

Section 17: UK Myths & Folklore

801. Who is the legendary king associated with the Round Table?
A) King Alfred
B) King Leopold
C) King Arthur
D) King James

802. What is the name of the wizard often associated with King Arthur?
A) Merlin
B) Gandalf
C) Saruman
D) Elminster

803. Which creature is said to inhabit the waters of Loch Ness in Scotland?
A) Kelpie
B) Dragon
C) Nessie
D) Selkie

804. In British folklore, what are "Will-o'-the-wisps"?
A) Goblins
B) Ghostly lights
C) Fairies
D) Witches

805. Which British folk hero is famous for robbing the rich to give to the poor?
A) Robin Hood
B) Dick Turpin
C) Hereward the Wake
D) Blackbeard

806. The Giant's Causeway in Northern Ireland is associated with which giant?
A) Fingal
B) Gargantua
C) Finn McCool
D) Polyphemus

807. What is the name of the sword in the stone in Arthurian legend?
A) Caladbolg
B) Clarent
C) Curtana
D) Excalibur

808. Which British creature is known for leading travelers astray?
A) Pixie
B) Puck
C) Black Dog
D) Changeling

809. What is the Glastonbury Tor known to be?
A) A dragon's lair
B) The entrance to Avalon
C) A fairy kingdom
D) A witch coven's meeting place

810. Which legendary creature is said to haunt the moors of Devon?
A) The Beast of Bodmin
B) The Hound of the Baskervilles
C) The Dartmoor Pony
D) The Exmoor Beast

811. Which creature in British folklore is known to wash the clothes of those about to die?
A) The Dullahan
B) The Banshee
C) The Bean Nighe
D) The Grim

812. What do you call a group of fairies in British folklore?
A) A coven
B) A troupe
C) A circle
D) A host

813. Lady Godiva famously rode through the streets of which city?
A) London
B) Coventry
C) York
D) Cambridge

814. What is the name of the benevolent Cornish spirit that is said to aid miners?
A) Tommyknocker
B) Bucca
C) Knockers
D) Bluecap

815. Which creature's gaze is said to turn people to stone?
A) Gorgon
B) Basilisk
C) Griffin
D) Wyvern

816. What type of mythical entity is Puck from "A Midsummer Night's Dream"?
A) Gargoyle
B) Troll
C) Fairy
D) Hobgoblin

817. Which British mythical being is known to be a shapeshifter and often a trickster?
A) Leprechaun
B) Brownie
C) Púca
D) Boggart

818. The Eildon Tree in Scottish folklore is associated with which legendary wizard?
A) Merlin
B) Michael Scot
C) Thomas Rhymer
D) Dallben

819. Who is the legendary outlaw associated with Sherwood Forest?
A) Robin Hood
B) Dick Turpin
C) William Tell
D) Captain Kidd

820. 'The Green Man' is a figure commonly found in which type of British structure?
A) Castles
B) Churches
C) Stone circles
D) Royal palaces

821. What is a Selkie in Scottish folklore?
A) A lake monster
B) A forest elf
C) A mountain giant
D) A sea spirit that can become human

822. Which folkloric character is known for wearing a red cap and killing travelers?
A) Brownie
B) Goblin
C) Redcap
D) Hobgoblin

823. In Welsh folklore, Annwn is known as what?
A) A mythical sword
B) The land of the living
C) The otherworld
D) A fearsome dragon

824. What was the quest of the Knights of the Round Table?
A) To find the Holy Grail
B) To rescue the princess
C) To slay the dragon
D) To reclaim Camelot

825. What is the name of the phantom black dog of East Anglia?
A) Barghest
B) Padfoot
C) Black Shuck
D) Cerberus

826. Which Welsh hero is associated with the phrase "Hiraeth", which speaks of deep longing?
A) King Arthur
B) Owain Glyndŵr
C) Llew Llaw Gyffes
D) Bran the Blessed

827. In the Arthurian legend, who was the mother of Sir Galahad?
A) Guinevere
B) Morgause
C) Elaine
D) Igraine

828. The Blarney Stone is said to bestow the gift of what?
A) Immortality
B) Eloquence
C) Invisibility
D) Eternal youth

829. Which legendary creature is known to lure young men to their deaths in rivers and streams?
A) Mermaid
B) Naiad
C) Jenny Greenteeth
D) Siren

830. The Cŵn Annwn are a type of what in Welsh mythology?
A) Underworld hounds
B) Wise old men
C) Magical horses
D) Forest spirits

Section 18: British Nostalgia

831. What was the name of the British children's TV series featuring a bear and a rag doll who live on a boat?
A) Rosie and Jim
B) Playdays
C) Tots TV
D) Brum

832. What is the name of the British science-fiction TV series that first aired in 1963?
A) The Avengers
B) Doctor Who
C) Blake's 7
D) Red Dwarf

833. Which coin ceased to be legal tender in 1984?
A) Half penny
B) Threepence
C) Sixpence
D) Shilling

834. What was the popular name for the Ford Sierra's shape when it was launched in 1982?
A) Teardrop
B) Jellymould
C) Aeroback
D) Wedge

835. Which TV series featured a home guard platoon during the Second World War?
A) Blackadder Goes Forth
B) Allo Allo
C) Dad's Army
D) It Ain't Half Hot Mum

836. What is the famous four-word catchphrase from the UK game show "Who Wants to Be a Millionaire"?
A) "Phone a friend now!"
B) "Is that your final answer?"
C) "Do you want to play?"
D) "Can I use a lifeline?"

837. Which of these sweets was a classic favorite in UK confectionery, particularly known for its television adverts featuring a boy and his dog?
A) Mars Bar
B) Milky Way
C) Cadbury's Dairy Milk
D) Bournville

838. What was the main colour of the original British passport before being changed to burgundy in the 1980s?
A) Blue
B) Green
C) Black
D) Red

839. Which of these British cars was famously known as 'The People's Car'?
A) Mini Cooper
B) Ford Escort
C) Volkswagen Beetle
D) Morris Minor

840. What is the name of the puppet monster that starred in a British TV show and famously disrupted interviews with his bad behavior?
A) Basil Brush
B) Zippy
C) Gordon the Gopher
D) Emu

841. Which British sitcom is set in the fictional holiday camp Maplins?
A) Hi-de-Hi!
B) Fawlty Towers
C) Are You Being Served?
D) The Good Life

842. In the 1980s, what was the name of the portable music player that let people to listen to music on the go?
A) Walkman
B) Boombox
C) Discman
D) MP3 player

843. Which British children's book series by Roger Hargreaves has been popular since the 1970s?
A) The Chronicles of Narnia
B) Harry Potter
C) Mr. Men and Little Miss
D) The Famous Five

844. What was the name of the clay animation character who first appeared on British television in 1959?
A) Wallace
B) Gromit
C) Morph
D) Pingu

845. Which British band was originally called "The Quarrymen"?
A) The Who
B) The Kinks
C) Led Zeppelin
D) The Beatles

846. What was the name of the leather-clad character played by Suzi Quatro in "Happy Days"?
A) Pinky Tuscadero
B) Leather Tuscadero
C) Joanie Cunningham
D) Jenny Piccalo

847. The British computer, the ZX Spectrum, was released in which year?
A) 1980
B) 1982
C) 1984
D) 1986

848. What was the title of the first James Bond film, released in 1962?
A) Goldfinger
B) From Russia with Love
C) Dr. No
D) Thunderball

849. Which of these was a popular drink in the UK during the 1970s and 80s, known for its distinctive bottle and advertising?
A) Tab Clear
B) Tizer
C) Cresta
D) Quatro

850. What was the name of the fictional British spy in the children's TV series "Danger Mouse"?
A) Agent 57
B) Secret Squirrel
C) Danger Mouse
D) Inspector Gadget

851. What was the title of the comedy sketch show that featured Rowan Atkinson and was a staple of 1980s British TV?
A. The Two Ronnies
B. Blackadder
C. Monty Python's Flying Circus
D. Not the Nine O'Clock News

852. Who was the female Prime Minister of the United Kingdom known as the "Iron Lady"?
A. Indira Gandhi
B. Angela Merkel
C. Margaret Thatcher
D. Theresa May

853. In the world of British comics, who is Dennis's dog in "The Beano"?
A. Gnasher
B. Gromit
C. Kipper
D. Snowy

854. Which of these British game shows had contestants racing around a supermarket?
A. Fun House
B. Supermarket Sweep
C. The Crystal Maze
D. The Price is Right

855. Which historical British event was marked by parties and celebrations in the street in 1977?
A. The end of WWII
B. The Queen's Silver Jubilee
C. The Moon landing
D. The wedding of Charles and Diana

856. Which iconic British band released "Bohemian Rhapsody" in 1975?
A. The Beatles
B. Queen
C. Led Zeppelin
D. Pink Floyd

857. Which children's TV show featured a character known as "The Soup Dragon"?
A. Rainbow
B. The Magic Roundabout
C. Clangers
D. Bagpuss

858. What was the name of the famous British ocean liner that was retired in 1967?
A. HMS Victory
B. RMS Titanic
C. RMS Queen Mary
D. SS Great Britain

Answers

UK Geography

1.	C) Ben Nevis
2.	A) River Severn
3.	C) Edinburgh
4.	D) Isle of Man
5.	A) Loch Ness
6.	B) Lowestoft Ness
7.	D) Aberdeen
8.	C) Cairngorms
9.	B) Wiltshire
10.	A) Cardiff
11.	B) Cambridge
12.	D) Kent
13.	C) Belfast
14.	C) Isle of Wight
15.	D) Northern Ireland
16.	A) The Roman Empire
17.	B) Northern Ireland
18.	B) River Mersey
19.	A) The Midlands
20.	B) Baths
21.	B) River Taff
22.	C) Four
23.	B) The North Sea
24.	A) Cornwall
25.	C) Lewis and Harris
26.	D) The Inner Hebrides
27.	A) Edinburgh
28.	B) Kent
29.	D) Snowdonia
30.	B) Somerset
31.	B) Liverpool

32.	A) Highlands
33.	C) Liverpool
34.	B) Solent
35.	B) Ireland
36.	A) Glasgow
37.	D) The East Midlands
38.	A) River Irwell
39.	B) Dorset and Devon
40.	C) Snowdonia
41.	C) Cardiff
42.	A) Wales
43.	C) The East Midlands
44.	D) Liverpool
45.	D) The Thames Estuary
46.	A) Edinburgh
47.	C) Wales
48.	B) Irish Sea
49.	D) Lough Neagh
50.	A) Devon
51.	A) River Bann
52.	B) Ireland
53.	A) Fort William
54.	C) Belfast
55.	A) Gloucestershire
56.	C) Manchester
57.	A) Devon
58.	A) Avon
59.	C) Scotland
60.	A) Avon
61.	C) Isle of Man
62.	D) University
63.	B) Dorset
64.	D) Northumberland
65.	A) Lancaster

UK History

66.	B) High taxes
67.	A) Queen Elizabeth I
68.	A) 1215
69.	B) The Gunpowder Plot
70.	C) Elizabeth I
71.	A) Henry VII
72.	D) Harold II and William the Conqueror
73.	A) 1086
74.	B) Neville Chamberlain
75.	B) Desire for a male heir
76.	A) Charles I
77.	D) Margaret Thatcher
78.	B) Scotland
79.	B) The Great Fire
80.	C) Potato
81.	D) Henry VIII
82.	B) James Cook
83.	B) Textiles
84.	D) Queen Victoria
85.	A) The Battle of Trafalgar
86.	D) Electoral reforms
87.	A) Edith Smith
88.	B) South Africa
89.	A) 1918
90.	B) Scotland
91.	C) Anglicanism
92.	C) The Jacobite Rebellions
93.	B) Robert Walpole
94.	D) Surat
95.	A) To extend the franchise to the middle classes
96.	B) George III
97.	B) Establishing a penal colony
98.	D) Emmeline Pankhurst

99.	C) The Magna Carta
100.	B) Anne
101.	C) Air
102.	A) The Mayflower
103.	A) Lancaster and York
104.	C) The Magna Carta
105.	B) James II
106.	D) George V
107.	D) The Hundred Years' War
108.	B) The Commonwealth
109.	B) Clement Attlee
110.	A) The Great Migration
111.	C) 14th
112.	A) Richard III
113.	B) Philip II of Spain
114.	A) Ireland
115.	B) Methodism
116.	D) Robert the Bruce
117.	D) Imported grain
118.	A) Anne Boleyn
119.	A) The Crimean War
120.	B) Charles II
121.	A) Thomas Arne
122.	A) Wat Tyler
123.	B) Chris Patten
124.	A) The Crystal Palace
125.	C) William the Conqueror
126.	A) Nancy Astor
127.	B) 1707
128.	A) James I
129.	B) Elizabeth I
130.	D) Harold Godwinson
131.	C) Textile
132.	B) Sir Francis Drake
133.	B) Scotland

134. D) Electoral reform
135. A) King Arthur
136. B) Manchester
137. B) Treaty of Paris
138. C) Postage stamp
139. A) Robin Hood
140. A) 1666
141. C) Palestine
142. A) 1919
143. B) Agricultural technology
144. B) China
145. D) Queen Elizabeth II
146. A) Admiral Nelson
147. B) Herbert Henry Asquith
148. D) The House of Commons
149. A) Duke of Wellington
150. B) Fascism
151. A) The criminal laws imposing harsh sentences
152. B) Egypt

British Royal Family

153. A) Buckingham Palace
154. B) Prince William
155. C) University of St Andrews
156. B) Diana Spencer
157. C) Prince of Wales
158. C) The Queen's Official Birthday
159. B) Prince Harry
160. B) Nairobi, Kenya
161. A) Prince George
162. D) Both B and C
163. C) Earl of Wessex
164. C) Sandhurst Military Academy
165. C) Princess Anne

166.	C) Queen Elizabeth
167.	A) Prince Edward
168.	A) Duke of Edinburgh
169.	D) Archie Harrison Mountbatten-Windsor
170.	C) Prince William
171.	B) 2012
172.	D) King George VI
173.	A) Sandringham House
174.	A) Duchess of Cambridge
175.	D) Trooping the Colour
176.	C) Prince Charles
177.	A) The Royal Foundation
178.	B) King George VI
179.	D) The Duke of Rothesay
180.	C) Four
181.	B) Princess Charlotte
182.	A) Duchess of Cornwall
183.	B) Prince Andrew
184.	A) Windsor Castle
185.	B) Queen Elizabeth II
186.	C) Queen Elizabeth II
187.	B) King George VI
188.	C) Mountbatten-Windsor
189.	B) Duchess of Cambridge
190.	B) Prince William
191.	B) Glamis Castle
192.	A) Peter Phillips
193.	C) Duke of Rothesay
194.	B) Prince William
195.	A) Princess Margaret
196.	D) Serena Armstrong-Jones
197.	B) Queen Elizabeth II
198.	A) The Halo Trust
199.	A) Zara Tindall
200.	C) King Edward VIII

201.   C) Prince Charles
202.   B) The Duke of Edinburgh Award

British Food & Drink

203.   B) Spotted Dick
204.   B) Barley
205.   A) Cheddar
206.   C) Lamb
207.   C) Shortcrust pastry
208.   B) Neeps and tatties
209.   D) Lager
210.   B) Cherry
211.   B) Chorizo
212.   B) Roast dinner
213.   A) Cod
214.   C) Cullen Skink
215.   C) Eton Mess
216.   C) Scones
217.   B) Tea
218.   C) Vanilla
219.   D) Pasta
220.   A) Christmas cake
221.   D) Heineken
222.   D) Pilchards or sardines
223.   D) Finger sandwich
224.   B) Crème brûlée
225.   C) Lamb
226.   B) Parkin
227.   A) Seaweed
228.   D) Leicestershire
229.   C) Ice cream
230.   A) Scotland
231.   B) Sandwich
232.   C) Aspic jelly

233. C) Cobbler
234. B) Gin
235. C) Trifle
236. D) Chicken
237. B) Marzipan
238. C) Cob
239. B) Marmite
240. B) Stout and Champagne
241. A) Cottage pie
242. D) A savory spread
243. C) Bergamot
244. A) Yorkshire pudding
245. C) Horseradish sauce
246. C) With clotted cream and jam
247. D) Margarita
248. C) Treacle tart

British Slang & Sayings

249. C) Amazed
250. B) It's excellent
251. A) Stay cheerful
252. C) Broke
253. C) Tired
254. A) Very pleased
255. B) Teasing or mocking someone
256. A) Suspicious or poor quality
257. B) Devastated or very disappointed
258. C) To take a quick look
259. D) Energetic
260. D) It's very expensive
261. C) They are not very intelligent or are behaving oddly
262. A) Surprise
263. B) Ordinary, with no frills
264. B) Annoyed
265. A) Fed up

266. A) Trying to find a romantic partner
267. D) Something going wrong
268. D) British pound sterling
269. C) To skip an obligation, especially school
270. B) In good order, going well
271. B) Cause a disturbance or problem
272. C) The whole thing, or everything that is possible
273. B) You are very tired
274. C) It's said when something is finished or completed easily
275. B) Eccentric or crazy
276. A) Very happy
277. B) To steal it
278. C) Extremely disappointed
279. C) To run away quickly
280. D) A casual conversation
281. A) Tasteless
282. D) A little hungry
283. A) Made a mess of something
284. A) Being dishonest or fraudulent
285. B) Stop talking or be quiet
286. B) To speak or write lengthily and without making much point
287. C) They have become irrational or are not thinking sensibly
288. C) The idea that if something can go wrong, it will
289. A) Sloshed
290. B) They are feeling unwell or not quite right
291. C) The police
292. C) They are alone
293. A) Lacking intelligence
294. B) They lack the will or desire to do something
295. C) You have made a profit
296. D) Pushing the limits of what is acceptable
297. B) Nonsense or foolish talk

British Sport

298. C) Andy Murray

299. C) Manchester

300. C) Liverpool

301. D) Graeme Obree

302. B) 1948

303. D) Wayne Rooney

304. A) Daley Thompson

305. B) Silverstone

306. A) Andrew Flintoff

307. C) Aintree Grand National

308. B) The Red Roses

309. D) Mike Hawthorn

310. A) Everton

311. B) 1

312. B) Adam Peaty

313. C) Wimbledon

314. B) Alastair Cook

315. B) On the Thames in Henley-on-Thames

316. A) Jonny Wilkinson

317. C) Paul Lawrie

318. A) Dario Franchitti

319. B) Tyson Fury

320. C) 4

321. A) 147

322. A) 1966

323. A) David Beckham

324. C) Kelly Holmes

325. B) Wentworth Club

326. A) Sir Chris Hoy

327. B) Tom Daley

328. B) Martin Johnson

329. B) Liverpool

330. D) Sir Mo Farah
331. C) Doncaster
332. D) Sir Stanley Matthews
333. B) 1981
334. A) Yellow
335. B) Peter Shilton
336. B) Manchester
337. A) 180
338. C) Nicola Adams
339. D) 2015
340. A) The Ashes Urn
341. A) Lewis Hamilton
342. A) Sheffield United
343. B) Fred Perry
344. A) River Thames
345. A) Clive Woodward
346. C) The Ashes
347. A) Paula Radcliffe

UK Flora & Fauna

348. C) Oak
349. B) Red Deer
350. A) Kingfisher
351. B) Cat
352. C) Japanese Knotweed
353. A) Lady's Smock
354. D) Both B and C
355. C) English Oak
356. A) Rana temporaria
357. D) All of the above
358. A) Starling
359. B) Coniferous forests
360. B) Butterfly
361. C) Water Vole

362. B) Plankton
363. D) Red-bellied Woodpecker
364. B) Chalk grasslands
365. C) Common Pipistrelle
366. B) Insects and worms
367. B) Adder
368. B) Snipe
369. C) Inflatable red throat pouch
370. A) Spanish Bluebell
371. C) White
372. D) Both A and B
373. A) Sundew
374. A) Hibernation
375. C) Small mammals and birds
376. A) Black Grouse
377. C) Lizard
378. B) Heathland
379. C) European toad
380. A) Otter
381. B) Butterfly
382. B) Sycamore
383. C) Devil's-bit Scabious
384. B) A breeding display area for birds
385. A) Grey Squirrel
386. A) Ants
387. D) All of the above
388. B) Singing at night
389. D) All of the above
390. C) Mustelidae (Weasel family)
391. B) It has a distinctive song.
392. B) Starfish
393. B) Broadleaved woodland
394. C) Small mammals and birds
395. B) Wet meadows
396. A) Dunes

397. D) Over 200 mph

British Art & Literature

398. B) Jane Austen
399. D) J.M.W. Turner
400. D) Hamlet
401. B) George Eliot
402. A) Romanticism
403. D) Dylan Thomas
404. A) John Everett Millais
405. B) George Orwell
406. A) London
407. C) David Copperfield
408. A) J.R.R. Tolkien
409. A) John William Waterhouse
410. D) Samuel Taylor Coleridge
411. D) Pride and Prejudice
412. C) Virginia Woolf
413. A) Hans Holbein the Younger
414. B) Arthur Conan Doyle
415. D) Mary Shelley
416. C) Alfred, Lord Tennyson
417. B) Jonathan Swift
418. C) Lord Byron
419. B) John Constable
420. A) Geoffrey Chaucer
421. C) Virginia Woolf
422. B) Jay Gatsby
423. A) Oscar Wilde
424. C) Graham Greene
425. D) George Frederick Watts
426. B) Elizabeth I
427. A) David Hockney
428. B) Dylan Thomas

429. C) Pride and Prejudice
430. A) William Blake
431. A) Evelyn Waugh
432. B) Antony Gormley
433. A) William Wordsworth
434. A) Stephen Hawking
435. A) The Modern Prometheus
436. C) Andrew Motion
437. A) Peter Blake
438. A) Pamela Andrews
439. C) John Keats
440. D) Samuel Beckett
441. D) J.M.W. Turner
442. B) London
443. A) London
444. B) Emma
445. D) Australia
446. B) The YBAs (Young British Artists)
447. D) The perils of totalitarianism
448. C) Oscar Wilde
449. A) John Constable
450. B) Emily Brontë

British Landmarks & Monuments

451. C) Stonehenge
452. B) London
453. A) Bath
454. A) The London Eye
455. D) London
456. A) Scotland
457. D) Bloomsbury
458. B) Castle Rock
459. D) Buckingham Palace
460. B) Berkshire

461. C) Kensington Palace
462. A) Newcastle
463. B) Its stone circle
464. B) Liverpool
465. B) William Wallace
466. D) The Mall
467. C) Wales
468. C) River Avon
469. A) South Kensington
470. B) Winston Churchill
471. C) Northern Ireland
472. D) RAF Coningsby
473. A) Portsmouth
474. B) Brighton
475. A) Cardiff
476. D) Scotland
477. C) The Eden Project
478. A) Lambeth Palace
479. B) York
480. C) Tintagel Castle
481. B) Lake District
482. A) Greenwich
483. D) Whitehall
484. B) University of Oxford
485. C) Regent's Park
486. D) York
487. D) Edinburgh
488. B) Dorset
489. A) Durham Cathedral
490. A) Oxfordshire
491. B) Wales
492. B) King Henry VIII
493. B) 1078
494. A) Nelson's Column
495. D) The British Museum

496. A) York
497. A) Oxford
498. B) Kensington Palace
499. C) River Thames
500. C) Stonehenge
501. B) Edinburgh Castle
502. C) The Iron Bridge
503. B) Big Ben
504. A) Falkirk
505. B) Sir Winston Churchill
506. C) Balmoral Castle
507. C) Whitehall
508. B) Tower Bridge
509. C) Northern Ireland
510. A) Manchester
511. A) Along the border with Scotland

Famous Brits

512. C) Octavia Hill
513. A) George Orwell
514. B) Margaret Thatcher
515. B) Alexander Fleming
516. D) Queen Victoria
517. D) The Beatles
518. A) Stephen Hawking
519. B) Geoffrey Chaucer
520. D) Daniel Craig
521. B) William Shakespeare
522. A) Florence Nightingale
523. D) Charles Darwin
524. A) Banksy
525. A) Adele
526. B) Neville Chamberlain
527. C) Arthur Conan Doyle

528. B) Dorothy Hodgkin
529. C) Mary Quant
530. D) Lewis Hamilton
531. C) Isaac Newton
532. A) Nancy Astor
533. C) Elton John
534. C) Stephen Hawking
535. B) Florence Nightingale
536. C) Bradley Wiggins
537. D) Jane Austen
538. B) Winston Churchill
539. B) Edward Elgar
540. D) Queen Victoria
541. C) J.R.R. Tolkien
542. B) Isaac Newton
543. C) James Cook
544. A) Alfred Hitchcock
545. D) Emma Watson
546. D) William Henry Bragg
547. C) Sacha Baron Cohen
548. D) Henry VIII
549. B) Winston Churchill
550. B) Tim Berners-Lee
551. B) Helen Mirren
552. A) Banksy
553. A) Robert Falcon Scott
554. C) King Arthur
555. C) Johnny Depp
556. A) Ian Fleming
557. A) King George III
558. B) Freddie Mercury
559. B) William Wilberforce
560. C) Francis Crick
561. A) Eddie Redmayne

British TV & Film

562.   B) Benedict Cumberbatch
563.   B) Slough
564.   A) Emmerdale
565.   B) Winston Graham
566.   C) Christopher Eccleston
567.   D) A country estate
568.   B) Claire Foy
569.   D) Fleabag (She is never given a proper name)
570.   C) Birmingham
571.   B) Danny Boyle
572.   B) 1950s
573.   A) Public Relations
574.   A) Tracey
575.   C) Baking
576.   D) Renée Zellweger
577.   D) World War I
578.   D) The staff of an IT support team
579.   C) Colin Firth
580.   B) Teenagers and their lives
581.   A) Brother
582.   C) Rowan Atkinson
583.   B) Police Detective
584.   A) Geraldine
585.   A) Steelworkers
586.   A) Torchwood
587.   B) Idris Elba
588.   C) The Daleks
589.   C) Danny Boyle
590.   C) Queen Anne
591.   C) A police detective
592.   B) A movie star
593.   A) Malia
594.   A) The Last Kingdom

595.   D) Daniel Craig
596.   B) The Winchester
597.   A) Keeping Up Appearances
598.   C) Gosford Park
599.   C) Jed Mercurio
600.   A) Charlie Brooker
601.   B) Robbie Coltrane
602.   A) Prestwich
603.   A) Cate Blanchett
604.   A) Reynholm Industries
605.   B) Mike Newell
606.   A) Arkwright's
607.   C) A village in Yorkshire
608.   A) David Tennant
609.   A) His secretary
610.   B) Edina
611.   B) Detective Chief Inspector
612.   D) Vince
613.   A) Bouquet
614.   A) Geraldine Granger
615.   B) Daniel Radcliffe

British Music

616.   C) The Beatles
617.   C) Jazz
618.   A) Wonderwall
619.   A) Ed Sheeran
620.   A) Gordon Sumner
621.   B) Queen
622.   A) 19
623.   C) The Kinks
624.   B) Ed Sheeran

625.	B) Amy Winehouse
626.	B) Spice Girls
627.	A) Blur
628.	A) Coldplay
629.	C) Face Value
630.	C) Elton John
631.	A) Pet Shop Boys
632.	A) Robbie Williams
633.	C) David Bowie
634.	B) Robert Plant
635.	B) Gala
636.	D) Robbie Williams
637.	B) Oasis
638.	B) Adele
639.	A) Morrissey
640.	A) The Cure
641.	B) Pulp
642.	A) Fleetwood Mac
643.	C) The Prodigy
644.	A) The Stone Roses
645.	B) Black Sabbath
646.	B) Led Zeppelin
647.	A) Depeche Mode
648.	B) "Bohemian Rhapsody" by Queen
649.	C) Amy Winehouse
650.	C) Duran Duran
651.	A) Genesis
652.	B) The Rolling Stones
653.	B) Kylie Minogue
654.	B) Sam Smith
655.	C) Radiohead
656.	C) David Bowie
657.	C) The Who
658.	C) Whatever People Say I Am, That's What I'm Not
659.	B) Iron Maiden

660. A) The Human League
661. A) Queen
662. A) Spice Girls
663. B) Pink Floyd
664. A) The Eurythmics
665. C) Sex Pistols

UK Holidays & Celebrations

666. B) Pancakes
667. A) St. David
668. C) The Gunpowder Plot of 1605
669. A) April 23
670. C) Poppy
671. B) The day after Christmas Day
672. B) December 25 - January 5
673. C) Bonfire Night
674. D) The Pancake Day Race
675. D) Edinburgh
676. A) The fourth Sunday in Lent
677. C) May Day
678. B) Caribbean
679. B) The Queen's official birthday
680. C) Trick-or-treating
681. C) Palm Sunday
682. C) Horticulture
683. B) Boxing Day
684. A) January 25
685. B) It honors the Queen's birthday.
686. B) Dance around the maypole
687. A) The third Sunday in June
688. A) Christmas
689. C) Stonehenge
690. B) Strawberries

691. C) It is a part of the Queen's official birthday celebrations.
692. A) The Gloucestershire Cheese Rolling
693. A) Around the time of the Harvest Moon, close to the autumn equinox
694. B) London
695. C) Hogmanay

British Inventions

696. B) Tim Berners-Lee
697. A) Frank Whittle
698. B) 1826
699. B) Shropshire
700. A) Jethro Tull
701. A) John Boyd Dunlop
702. B) World War II
703. C) The Analytical Engine
704. B) 1863
705. A) Edward Jenner
706. A) 1668
707. D) Alexander Fleming
708. A) John Harrison
709. A) Alexander Graham Bell
710. C) The Aileron
711. D) John Hobbins
712. D) John Kemp Starley
713. D) 1831
714. C) Charles Macintosh
715. D) Elisha Gray
716. B) George Stephenson
717. C) Fry's
718. C) John C. Taylor
719. B) 1829

720. C) 1843
721. A) John Logie Baird
722. A) Sir Christopher Cockerell
723. B) John Shepherd-Barron
724. A) Hubert Cecil Booth
725. B) 1766
726. C) 1863
727. A) Thomas Allbutt
728. B) 1830
729. A) Alastair Pilkington
730. A) John Montagu
731. A) Robert W. Paul
732. D) Samuel Taylor
733. D) Bristol
734. A) 1837
735. B) William Howard Livens
736. A) Sir Barnes Wallis
737. B) 1804
738. A) Christopher Latham Sholes
739. B) 1933
740. C) 1934

British World Records

741. B) J.K. Rowling
742. C) Tom Harrison
743. D) 146 kilograms
744. A) Helen Sharman
745. C) Status Quo
746. B) 70.8 mph
747. C) 443
748. A) Michael Fish
749. D) 10,540 pounds
750. B) Trevor Baylis
751. D) More than 300

752.	B) 7 feet (2.13 meters)
753.	A) 18.29 meters
754.	C) 310.6 mph
755.	D) 40,000
756.	C) Victor Vescovo
757.	A) 1,198
758.	B) 14.531 seconds
759.	B) Mark Beaumont
760.	D) 77 years
761.	B) Coronation Street
762.	C) George Atkinson
763.	A) Trevor McDonald
764.	A) 40 days
765.	D) 400,000
766.	D) From London to Gibraltar
767.	B) 2 meters
768.	C) Wagner's Ring Cycle
769.	A) Tim Peake
770.	A) 8 ft 1 in

UK Guess The Year

771.	A) 1066
772.	A) 1952
773.	B) 1215
774.	C) 1666
775.	D) 1973
776.	D) 1694
777.	B) 1912
778.	A) 1918
779.	B) 1940
780.	B) 1967
781.	A) 1863
782.	C) 1973
783.	B) 1971

784. B) 1994
785. A) 1780
786. C) 1966
787. B) 1851
788. B) 1564
789. C) 1936
790. A) 1948
791. C) 1978
792. B) 1688
793. B) 1982
794. D) 1986
795. D) 1986
796. A) 1959
797. A) 1952
798. B) 1985
799. C) 1979
800. B) 2000

UK Myths & Folklore

801. C) King Arthur
802. A) Merlin
803. C) Nessie
804. B) Ghostly lights
805. A) Robin Hood
806. C) Finn McCool
807. D) Excalibur
808. C) Black Dog
809. B) The entrance to Avalon
810. B) The Hound of the Baskervilles
811. C) The Bean Nighe
812. D) A host
813. B) Coventry
814. B) Bucca
815. B) Basilisk

816. D) Hobgoblin
817. C) Púca
818. A) Merlin
819. A) Robin Hood
820. B) Churches
821. D) A sea spirit that can become human
822. C) Redcap
823. C) The otherworld
824. A) To find the Holy Grail
825. C) Black Shuck
826. B) Owain Glyndŵr
827. C) Elaine
828. B) Eloquence
829. C) Jenny Greenteeth
830. A) Underworld hounds

British Nostalgia

831. A) Rosie and Jim
832. B) Doctor Who
833. A) Half penny
834. B) Jellymould
835. C) Dad's Army
836. B) "Is that your final answer?"
837. C) Cadbury's Dairy Milk
838. A) Blue
839. C) Volkswagen Beetle
840. C) Gordon the Gopher
841. A) Hi-de-Hi!
842. A) Walkman
843. C) Mr. Men and Little Miss
844. C) Morph
845. D) The Beatles
846. B) Leather Tuscadero
847. B) 1982

848. C) Dr. No
849. C) Cresta
850. C) Danger Mouse
851. D) Not the Nine O'Clock News
852. C) Margaret Thatcher
853. A) Gnasher
854. B) Supermarket Sweep
855. B) The Queen's Silver Jubilee
856. B) Queen
857. C) Clangers
858. C) RMS Queen Mary

Printed in Great Britain
by Amazon